ROUTLEDGE LIBRARY EDITIONS: HUMAN RESOURCE MANAGEMENT

Volume 7

TIME, WORK AND ORGANIZATION

TIME, WORK AND ORGANIZATION

PAUL BLYTON, JOHN HASSARD,
STEPHEN HILL AND KEN STARKEY

Routledge
Taylor & Francis Group

LONDON AND NEW YORK

First published in 1989 by Routledge

This edition first published in 2017
by Routledge
2 Park Square, Milton Park, Abingdon, Oxon OX14 4RN

and by Routledge
711 Third Avenue, New York, NY 10017

Routledge is an imprint of the Taylor & Francis Group, an informa business

British Library Cataloguing in Publication Data
A catalogue record for this book is available from the British Library

ISBN: 978-1-138-80870-6 (Set)
ISBN: 978-1-315-18006-9 (Set) (ebk)
ISBN: 978-1-138-28919-2 (Volume 7) (hbk)
ISBN: 978-1-315-26727-2 (Volume 7) (ebk)

Publisher's Note
The publisher has gone to great lengths to ensure the quality of this reprint but points out that some imperfections in the original copies may be apparent.

Disclaimer
The publisher has made every effort to trace copyright holders and would welcome correspondence from those they have been unable to trace.

TIME, WORK, AND ORGANIZATION

Time, Work and Organization

Paul Blyton, John Hassard, Stephen Hill, and Ken Starkey

ROUTLEDGE
London and New York

First published in 1989
by Routledge
11 New Fetter Lane, London EC4P 4EE
29 West 35th Street, NY 10001, New York

© 1989 Paul Blyton, John Hassard, Stephen Hill, and Kenneth Starkey

Phototypeset in 10pt Times Roman by
Mews Photosetting, Beckenham, Kent
Printed and bound in Great Britain by
Billings & Sons Limited, Worcester.

British Library Cataloguing in Publication Data

Blyton, Paul, *1953-* .
    Time, work, and organization.
    1. Work patterns
    I. Title
    331.25'7

    ISBN 0-415-00418-7

Library of Congress Cataloging-in-Publication Data

Time, work, and organization / Paul Blyton . . . [et al.].
        p.   cm.
    Bibliography: p.
    Includes indexes.
    ISBN 0-415-00418-7 : $55.00 (U.S.)
    1. Time study. 2. Time management. I. Blyton, Paul.
T60.4.T55   1988
658.5'421 — dc19   88-30647
                                                                CIP

Contents

Contents

Figures

Tables

Tables

Preface

Multi-disciplinary approaches to particular areas of study certainly sound as though they ought to be a 'good thing'. Nowhere more than in the investigation of work and organization does the artificiality of academic boundaries show itself as an administrative convenience rather than a reflection of reality. Yet relatively few multi-disciplinary studies (not to mention the intellectual no-man's-land of inter-disciplinary studies) actually pay rich dividends; the common denominator is often too low to generate a satisfying learning experience either for researcher or audience.

It is of course for the reader to judge whether the present venture has been worthwhile. In five principal chapters we have sought to highlight some of the major themes in the study of time and work within separate but related fields of study. In the introduction and conclusions a number of the common starting points and issues are examined, together with the various conclusions which different researchers have drawn in the process of running their quarry to earth.

Working together, the four authors have enriched their individual understanding of worktime through exposure to approaches taken by others working within different discipline boundaries. The endeavour has been very much a joint one, and the ordering of authors' names is simply alphabetical. Admittedly, many gaps and disjunctions in the text remain; this is despite all the efforts made by Kath Hollister at UWIST (University of Wales Institute of Science and Technology), who retyped the final manuscript to make it look at least presentably coherent. The authors would like to add their thanks to Sudi Sharifi for the efficient preparation of the subject index.

P.B.
J.H.
S.H.
K.S.

1

Introduction

Time is one of the central preoccupations in contemporary industrial society: enormous effort is expended in designing ways to increase the amount of activity which can be done in a given time. The pace of life in modern society and the emphasis placed on such values as growth, success, advancement and gain has put a premium on time. Time not spent profitably is time 'lost'. Its quintessentially finite nature has keened the edge of its preoccupation (the time taken to read these words has already gone forever).

Despite its importance, a generally accepted definition of time remains elusive. Compounding the problem of definition are the many ways of experiencing time — the many different ways in which time is 'experienced and handled by collectivities' (Zerubavel 1981: xii). Yet, despite this multiplicity, it is the contention of a growing body of research into social time that social life is structured and regulated at a fundamental level by its temporal parameters. Different cultures are characterized by different value systems which impact on attitudes to and experiences of time. In a complex society composed of a vast array of collectivities, there are differing value systems relating to the temporal aspects of human existence. Yet, despite these differences, research into social time is beginning to establish that, for our industrial society, a primary determinant of the experience of and attitudes to time is the experience of work (Grossin 1974). In short, work provides 'the guidelines by which adults ordinarily structure their use of time' (Calkins 1969–70; 487). The kind of work individuals are in, the kind of work-organizations they belong to, assume a primary importance when it comes to issues concerning individual and collective time.

A key feature of work-organizations as we know them is the prevalence of clock-time. An over-arching temporal concern is

1

generated by our dependence on the clock for the smooth functioning of our organizations (Moore 1963a). The clock serves as a crucial technology for co-ordination and control. The ubiquity of clocks, the constant presence of clock-time, the use of clock-time as an organizing device according to which we schedule our waking lives, the ways in which clock-time filters into non-work time, reflect the dominant western conception of time as a commodity. The commodification of time leads inexorably to a sense of time as a quantity in short supply. Time becomes a crucial resource as important as money. Indeed, it is often identified with money as in the phrase 'time is money'. The antithesis of clock-time is 'event-time' or 'task-time', when the event or task makes temporal demands which are not amenable to the logic of commodification or the rigidity the clock imposes.

Durkheim was the first to argue that the origins of time are social. Drawing his conclusions from the evidence of studies of primitive societies, he concluded that 'The foundation of the category of time is the rhythm of social life' (Durkheim 1976: 22). He was thus the first to focus on the collective social aspect of temporality. Time is not, as Kant held, a universal category inherent in the mind. It is essentially a 'collective representation', arising from the experience of the collectivity. Society provides the framework according to which time is arranged and crucial elements of this framework in modern western society are work and the clock. Primitive societies arrange their temporal frameworks according to the 'periodical recurrence of rites, feasts, and public ceremonies' (Durkheim 1976: 32); therefore time in primitive societies depends on the rhythms of nature and the repetition of natural events, not on clock or calendar.

Attitudes to and experience of time are conditioned by social life, particularly by membership of an occupational group. Time at work has to be understood within the context of a western culture with the dominant perspective of an economic orientation to time. This tends towards time's rationalization and commodification. The evolution of the organization of time at work and the way in which it is presently organized can only be understood in the context of the development of the Spirit of Capitalism (Weber 1952) which has created the chronic search for the most productive form of time-discipline at work. Since Marx, an influential view of work under capitalism has argued that management, as the agent of capital, has used the instrument of commodification to discipline labour and intensify its efforts at work by using time more productively. It is the capitalist system which has led to the commodification of time.

Developments in work organization, following particularly the scientific management studies of Taylor (Rose 1982), have promoted the continuing search for the most efficient use of time. Work is increasingly subject to rationalization and workers' time managed according to a 'relentless, calculating search for productive efficiency' (Hill 1981: 8). Industrial and bureaucratic time-discipline aim at order based on a process of routinization (Giddens 1979: 192). There is systematic pressure towards the more intensive use of time as part of the chronic search for improved efficiency. As a result, workers' control over their time at work is progressively reduced. The control of time becomes an essential feature of the power struggle between capital and labour. Control of and competition about time are key issues. Time at work ceases to be organized and measured according to events and the activities that constitute them. Work is subjected to the impersonal schedule and monitored by reference to the implacable clock. The beginning and ending of activities are subject to the necessities of time-slots. Submission to time 'is the price of modernization, productivity, potential affluence' (Landes 1983: 360). Time, as a result, presents itself not only as a control mechanism but as a central commodity. In the search for optimum productivity, the availability of time becomes the 'criterion of scarcity. . . . The organization, coordination and allocation of time . . . become the main problems' (Gunnell 1970: 84). Time at work ceases to be organized according to the demands of the task. The clock becomes dominant.

The commodified approach to time has been highlighted as of crucial significance to the way much work is organized. The commodification of time is seen by Giddens as a key feature of modern society. It holds the key:

> to the deepest transformations of day-to-day social life that are brought about by the emergence of capitalism. These relate both to the central phenomenon of the organization of production processes, and to the 'work-place', and also the intimate texture of how daily social life is experienced.
>
> (Giddens 1981: 130–1).

It is the 'buying and selling of time' that is one of 'the most distinctive features of modern capitalism' (Giddens 1984: 144). As time was commodified it 'became regarded as a scarce and exploitable resource' (Giddens 1979: 201).

Marx identified the commodification of time as a guiding principle of capitalism. One of the key themes of *Capital* is that, 'The economic

3

order of capitalism depends upon the exact control of time' (Giddens 1979: 210) and that the regulation, and exploitation, of labour-time is central to the economic development of the capitalist system. The logic of capitalist development entails the maximization of productivity in time, either by the lengthening of the working day or, when this becomes impossible, by the intensification of available time. It is a central Marxist argument that as hours of work decrease management compensates by intensifying the pace of work, employing such means as stricter supervision, incentive payment schemes, and technological innovation. Reduction in hours of work:

> Gives an immense impetus to the development of productivity and the more economic use of the conditions of production. It imposes on the worker an increased expenditure of labour within a time which remains constant, a heightened tension of labour power, and a closer filling-up of the pores of the working day, i.e. a condensation of labour, to a degree which can only be attained within the limits of the shortened working day. This compression of a greater mass of labour into a given period now counts for what it really is, namely an increase in the quantity of labour. In addition to the measure of its 'extensive magnitude', labour-time now acquires a measure of its intensity, or degree of density. The denser hour of the ten-hour working day contains more labour, i.e. expended labour-power, than the more porous hour of the twelve-hour working day.
>
> (Marx 1976: 534)

Time becomes everything, 'Man is nothing; he is, at most, the carcase of time.' This, Marx proclaims, is the central fact of modern industry (Marx and Engels 1976: 127). As much of the lifetime as possible of the labouring class, is converted by the economic pressure of the capitalist class into labour-time.

Capitalism contracts 'the pores of the working day' (Fenton 1984: 59), reducing all time to the influence of the 'cash nexus' (Hill 1981: 20). The imposition of time-discipline by management increases the density of working time. The scarcity of time as a resource, and aims by management to intensify time use at work — applying the measure of time use as an indicator of productivity — set the stage for a struggle between management and labour over temporal issues. A common site for this struggle has been the issue of piecework and the setting of rates of wages for levels of production that are considered equitable by both management and labour. Another major source of dispute has

4

been the length and organization of the working day. One of the most bitter recent industrial disputes in the United Kingdom, between the British Rail Board and the Associated Society of Locomotive Engineers and Footplatemen (ASLEF), concerned the latter issue. ASLEF resisted a major reorganisation of their working day (Starkey 1988a).

The way in which railway time has developed illustrates some of the key issues concerning time, work and organization. The railway worker has been subjected to as unrelenting a time discipline as any other group of workers, reflecting the importance of the adherence to one particular time framework in the efficient and safe operation of the rail system. Time has always been a central focus of railway culture as seen, for example, in the emphasis on the possession of an accurate timepiece. As long ago as 1939, Cottrell, in his seminal paper 'Time and the railroader', argued that the importance of time to the efficient running of the railway system deeply marked the whole of the railroader's life, working and non-working. The rigidity of the timetable, the system's subconscious mind, and the unrelenting time-discipline it demanded, created an over-arching scheme that controlled all of the railroader's life. The railroader became a 'slave to the clock; intense time-consciousness marks the railroader in all his social relationships. . . . The obverse of this occupational dependence on the clock is the almost complete denial of the opportunity to time-plan other relationships' (Cottrell 1939: 195–6).

The work Cottrell refers to is the American railroad system. McKenna (1980) makes broadly similar points concerning the evolution and effects of time discipline on railway work in the United Kingdom, emphasizing the 'tyranny of time' and the 'clock-and-watch-bound bondage' of the railway worker's 'roped existence' (McKenna 1980: 250). Struggles over the length of the working week on the railways led to an intensification of time use through such innovations as the big-engine policy — 'bigger, longer, heavier, faster'. If time itself could not be made available in 'bigger, longer' quantities, it could be employed more productively. Time, thus, comes to be experienced as faster and weighing more heavily on the worker operating according to new temporal demands.

Gurvitch contrasts the different attitudes to time of management and workers. Time is always too short for the former and too long for the latter. Management tries to master time in order to prolong it while workers try to master time in order to shorten it (Gurvitch 1964: 44). Industrial progress brought a new managerial time-discipline, an intensification of working time which rendered it

5

'denser, heavier, more tiring' (Grossin 1969: 163–4). Work organization came to depend increasingly upon 'the highly rationalized and
structured orders of formal and quantitative time' (Gunnell 1970: 82).
Time-keeping led to time-accounting, time-rationing and abstract time
(Mumford 1973). Grossin sees rigidity as the dominant characteristic
of modern work. Previously time was subordinated to task. Now this
relationship is reversed. Modern work typically involves:

> Rigidity, precision, compartmentalization of the time structures
> of work. . . . [Work] activities are firmly fixed in pre-prepared
> pigeon-holes that have to be filled. Industry thus separates time
> and task. Time assigns task. Arriving at work, the worker has in
> front of him a prepared network of measured times and . . .
> repetitive tasks. These make up separate equal periods according
> to which he assigns his movements without any choice in the matter.
> (Grossin 1974: 376)

A key outcome of the application of clock-time to work organization is the timetable. The timetable serves as a fundamental device
for organizing work. Work activity is regulated by the timetable's
division of the day, the week, and the year, into a sequence of set
tasks to be performed in specified time-slots. Each organization has
a set of rules, implicit or explicit, that governs how employees use
their time. These rules have not been closely examined. Clock-time
determines the parameters of the timetable and provides a measure
of activity. Timetablers, a little-researched group, have as their essential function the co-ordination of complex activity, specifying what
activities are to occur and how long they last (Starkey 1986). The
timetable acts as a habit system or unconscious mind for organizational
members (Cottrell 1939). It consists of a two-dimensional matrix of
events and time-slots, 'a set of blocks of time within which events
are durationally fixed, sequentially ordered and located between
absolute points in time' (Zerubavel 1976: 88–9). It sets out the work's
temporal framework, specifying 'geometry' (the limits on working
time in terms of hours and days worked) and 'substance' (the content
of these hours) (Grossin 1974: 127). Different forms of work differ
in the specificity of their timetables but some form of timetable is
an essential and, therefore, ubiquitous feature of the work situation.
Timetables reflect the rationalization of time use and the scarcity of
time as a basic work resource.

Differences in the specificity of timetables remind us of a fact
that the prevalence of the commodified view of time can obscure. As

Grossin (1974) points out, the degree of submission to the clock, timetables based on clock-time and how these timetables are imposed and time-discipline managed vary according to form of work. There is a heterogeneity of work situations, differing in their degree of temporal constraint. Different groups of workers exhibit what Gurvitch (1964) calls a spectrum of social times. Heterogeneity leads to multiple manifestations of time. Occupational groups can, then, be seen, in a Durkheimian sense, as constituting a 'multiplicity' of 'loci of sociotemporal orders' (Zerubavel 1979: 106). The temporal demands of professional work, for example, differ from those in unskilled work.

A dominant image of the professional is that of a member of an occupational group which is free to organize its work in the way it best sees fit. According to this view, professionals are an occupational group with a high degree of temporal autonomy (Grossin 1974). The professional is seen as escaping from the trend towards clock-based ways of organizing time because professional work is not amenable to the sort of precise measurement and specification this form of organization depends upon. Professional work, therefore, is still task-based.

Whether this view of professional work is accurate need not concern us here. (The issue of the nature of professional time has been dealt with elsewhere; see Starkey 1986.) The important point for this introduction is that the dominant view of the professional illustrates the fact that different work situations produce different experiences of time because time in these situations is organized differently. But different forms of work do have one important fact in common. Working time provides structure for individual lives. We are faced with a central paradox concerning work. Despite dissatisfaction and complaints concerning work and its time demands this structuring effect is desirable and even necessary. People generally prefer the state of being in work to the condition of being out of work. It appears that filled and structured time is of crucial psychological importance. People find too much empty, unfilled time intolerable. Work, with its career tracks and temporal benchmarks, serves an important function in guiding us through our passage in time (Roth 1963). In periods of enforced inactivity and lack of temporal structure, for example, at times of illness or unemployment, people tend to lose their grasp on time with deleterious psychological results (Roth 1963; Calkins 1969–70; Jahoda 1979). Some forms of work, too, can be too undemanding, generating a condition of underload. Conversely, work can provide too much structure and can, thus, become over-demanding, generating a condition of overload. Both

7

overload and underload at work are implicated in the incidence of occupational stress.

THE STRUCTURE OF THE BOOK

An organization behaviour perspective suggests that various levels of analysis have to be combined to understand the work situation and the experience of time by the individual in the organization. These levels of analysis are the individual, the organizational, the sociopolitical and the economic. Individual factors such as personality affect the experience of time. Individuals' attitudes to time are conditioned by membership of occupational groups and, although they are not necessarily aware of it, by wider sociocultural trends. The new industrial sociology argues that work organization cannot be adequately explored by looking only at the work-place level and that the sociopolitical context of work-place behaviour needs to be examined (Hill 1981). To understand the relationship between time, work and organization we need, therefore, to situate the individual in an occupational, organizational, sociopolitical and socio-economic context. An adequate analysis of the experience of time and its determinants has to examine the interplay between individual experience, membership of occupational group, the work situation in particular organizations and the context in which the work organization is situated, its environment. Individual and workgroup experience has to be related to the ways in which organizations manage time and to the ways organizations relate to their environment that affect working time within the organization. Time is not just a scarce resource for individuals. Organizations, too, can be short of time and they manage time scarcity in differing ways that impact on individual experience, which is mediated by membership of a particular occupational group. Time within organizations is a political issue. Groups negotiate about time, seeking to impose their definitions of the best ways of organizing time on other interest groups. Views of time function as 'solidifiers of group affiliations and as mechanisms of establishing and consolidating social boundaries between groups' (Zerubavel 1979: xxi).

An adequate perspective on time, work and organization, therefore, has to encompass psychological, social psychological, sociological, industrial relations and economic aspects of time as they affect work and organization. It is this perspective that this book sets out to develop. Chapter two deals with time and industrial sociology. It

8

argues that time is a missing variable in industrial sociology, which has tended to concentrate on structural factors at the expense of temporal dimensions. Industrial sociology, therefore, has tended to be 'time-free'. Where it has addressed time it has tended to do so in a very restrictive fashion, treating time as quantitative and homogeneous, rather than qualitative and heterogeneous. Working-time operates according to rhythms of experience, structured by members of organizations. The chapter goes on to argue for a social-anthropological perspective, focusing particularly on the distinction between the two major metaphors used to describe industrial time — 'line' and 'cycle'. From this analysis the chapter draws out the predominance of the linear metaphor in the analysis of industralism, one of the main byproducts of which is the notion of commodification. Finally, the argument is made for qualifying the standard linear-commodification thesis as a mode of analysis. This thesis is seen to overstate the rationality of production practices and understate the role of the social construction of temporal meanings. It tends to gloss over the fact that the industrial world is not composed simply of machine-paced work but includes a wealth of work processes based on self-paced production. Industrial time is much richer than the time portrayed in industrial sociology.

Chapter three addresses the psychology and social psychology of time at work. Cognitive psychology presents an information-processing view of temporal experience which is more useful for understanding work than a biological perspective. Construing the experience of time in terms of information-processing and the content of the information processed leads to a way of understanding time in terms of three basic dimensions — duration, intensity and pace. These help us to organize the literature on the experience of work, a key guiding principle of which is the concept of 'temporal constraint'. Occupations differ fundamentally in terms of this principle. The chapter goes on to consider the literature on occupational stress. Stress occurs when duration, intensity and pace of work are experienced as over- or under-demanding. Stress is generated by both underload and overload. Time out of work is particularly stressful and difficult to cope with. The chapter considers the experience of time out of work in periods of lengthy illness and long-term unemployment. The chapter ends by analysing a key mediating factor between individual and occupational group — commitment. If membership of occupational group and the social experience of work have a central effect on the experience of time, individual experience of work is conditioned by degree of commitment to the work situation and to occupational group.

Chapter four analyses working time from an economic perspective. Traditional economic theory sees leisure time and income from work (and hence work-time) as substitutable elements in the generation of satisfaction. The actual choice of working hours depends on the interaction of available opportunities with the preferences of potential employees. Various extensions of the theory have been developed, taking account of the productivity variations amongst different work-time profiles, between different employees and between different forms of capital. The economic analysis of work has as its mirror image the analysis of capital utilization. Planned underutilization of capital occurs because of rhythmic variations in other input prices and because of differences in the institutions of factor ownership. However, economic theory fails to yield unambiguous predictions about the effects on working time of rises in hourly wage rates. Developments in the economic analysis of working time involve the extension of economic principles to cover non-work time, subdivided into household production activities and leisure time. The working-time decision is then just one subset of total time allocation. The chapter concludes by considering recent developments in the economics of time allocation which analyse the lifetime allocation of work-time, concentrating on education, training and different time profiles of productivity and, therefore, reward.

Chapter five addresses the issue of time and organization, starting from a consideration of time as a boundary condition for defining and stabilizing existence. The limits of natural cycles give human beings the sense that time is a major element in the organization of existence. Particularly important among natural cycles is the diurnal or circadian rhythm. This cycle is linked, through the concept of entrainment, to issues of work organization. It is the notion of entrainment which links physiological cycles and industrial wellbeing — demonstrating, for example, the physiological consequences of shift and task cycles. During social development, time is an important factor in the structuring of basic human needs and, therefore, a key element in the process of socialization. The temporal parameters of human action become modified. There is a crucial shift from their basis in biological rhythms to the bases of the rhythms of formal organizations such as the family, the school and, eventually, the work-place. These establish the parameters of time-discipline. The proper timing of actions becomes a matter of response to social rules. Social behaviour is organized behaviour and comes to depend for its orderly qualities on common definitions, assumptions and actions with regard to the location of events in time. The structure of social time and,

10

ultimately of organizations, is based on three factors: synchronization, sequencing and rate of activity. A primary tool for considering passages through organizations is the notion of career which serves as a normative 'time chart' for organizational members. Self-concepts are based, fundamentally, on career time. The chapter concludes by analysing the three main time problems that organizations must solve: the reduction of temporal uncertainty; inter-unit conflicts of interest over temporal matters; and the inevitable scarcity of time. In a very real sense, one could argue that organizations owe their very existence to the need for collectivities to solve these three problems. In the search for solutions three main temporal concerns emerge: the need for time schedules; the need for synchronization; and, the need for time allocation. The chapter concludes by analysing some ways in which these organizational time problems have been addressed.

Chapter six looks at the important link between time and industrial relations. Together with wages, working time has represented a central issue in the development of industrial relations. Labour is typically purchased in temporal units. Trade unions have traditionally concentrated on regulating the duration of working-time. The intensity of working-time has tended to be dealt with at the less formal, local level and at the level of the workgroup. With the recent exceptions of the United States and Japan, basic weekly hours of work in industrial countries have tended to decline in a steplike fashion, from a 48 to a 44, then 42, 40 and 39-hour week. This decline has been regulated by both legislation and collective agreements. Falls in working hours are more likely at times of union strength and low inflation, the latter reducing pressures on maximizing wage increases. However, measures of actual hours of work have also to take into account over-time levels. These differ markedly from country to country and in the United Kingdom overtime hours remain high, despite recent attempts by managements to reduce overtime by more 'flexible' work arrangements. The distribution of working hours through the week is also affected by shiftwork patterns, which too have undergone a number of changes in recent years. Besides changes in the pattern of the working week, there are also changes in the pattern of the working year and working lifetime. Holidays and the availability of early retirement have increased. There has also been an increased emphasis on achieving greater flexibility in working-time. Here we see a shift from the 1970s' emphasis on flexibility for the benefit of both employers and employees to a more explicit focus on employer needs. The key issue here is the matching of technological and numerical/functional flexibility with temporal flexibility. Shiftwork is increasing and new forms of shiftwork (for example, four and five-crew working) are being introduced. Further reductions in working time are likely to be linked to more flexible patterns of worktime, with, for example, the increased individualization of worktime through annual hours contracts, variable shiftwork and rostering arrangements and multiple part-time schedules.

2

Time and industrial sociology

John Hassard

INTRODUCTION

This chapter examines how time and temporality have been
portrayed in industrial sociology. It outlines the main theories of
time available to sociologists, and suggests that these, when applied
in formal research investigations, can yield rich and diverse insights
into work behaviour. By drawing upon major figures in the sociology of time — such as Emile Durkheim, Mircea Eliade, Georges
Gurvitch, Wilbert Moore and Pitirm Sorokin — we note not only some
of the major differences between their positions, but also how
such differences, when contrasted systematically, offer a basis for
appreciating time as a qualitative as well as quantitative, cyclic as
well as linear, and heterogeneous as well as homogeneous,
phenomenon.[1]

However, in developing this analysis we note also how sociologists have for too long concentrated on quantitative explanations
of time at the expense of qualitative ones. We document how
the sociology of time has been informed, almost exclusively, by
a realist ontology, and how this has found expression in the development of nomothetic methods and positivist explanations. Dominant
images emerge from two, primarily positivist, traditions: functionalist studies of time structuring: and Marxian studies of temporal
commodification. Both invoke essentially linear time perspectives
and draw heavily on economic rationality (e.g. studies of time
budgets and time and motion). In contrast, studies which access
the heterogeneous and recursive nature of time, and which are
influenced by the metaphor of the 'cycle', are scarce. Few writers
document how actors experience working time as qualititative
and heterogeneous; that is, how they obtain meaning through the

recurrence of temporally-ordered events, and how they construct their own time reckoning systems.

Therefore, to correct this situation we discuss below work not only from the linear-quantitative tradition but also from the cyclic-qualitative one. First, on developing a conceptual framework, we offer explanations of working-time from the dominant linear-quantitative tradition. We draw upon theories of working-time in social history to explain how the economic structures of industrialism give rise to a range of linear metaphors which later influence the time perceptions of modern societies. This analysis provides a basis for illustrating how a linear-quantitative paradigm has become the dominant one in the sociology of time. Second, on recognising the importance of the linear tradition, we suggest nevertheless that for industrial sociology this does not provide a sufficient basis for explaining working-time. In particular, the linear tradition neglects the phenomenology of working-time, which in many respects draws upon cyclic metaphors. On turning to the French and American traditions in the sociology of time, we show the affinity between cyclic and qualitative time notions. We draw upon this relationship for explaining the subjective perception of working-time and develop this, empirically, by reference to anthropological studies of occupations. The chapter is brought to a conclusion when we make a case for developing a cyclic-qualitative paradigm for work-time research.

THE CONCEPT OF TIME

To develop this analysis, it is important that we first construct a conceptual framework. To achieve this, we draw upon some of the main images of time in social philosophy, and then upon two of the main time metaphors in social theory. These concerns are then brought together in the main body of the chapter.[2]

Social Philosophy

In philosophy, there is a long and sophisticated tradition of temporal analysis. The concept of time has, as Jaques (1982: xi) notes, been a central and continuous subject for philosophers for over two thousand years. Debate is found at a number of abstract levels, ranging from ontological concerns with time and existence, to epistemological concerns with time and understanding. It is a tradition which has yielded a wealth of abstract, complex yet unresolved questions.[3]

Although a detailed analysis of such questions is beyond our scope, we can at least note the main issues which confront the philosopher of time. To achieve this, we turn to the excellent introduction to temporal philosophy presented by Heath (1956). Heath introduces the philosophy of time by asking three questions central to discussions in the field. First, at the level of ontology, he asks whether we should regard time as an objective facticity 'out there' in the external world, or as a subjective essence which is constructed via a 'network of meanings'; that is, should we think of time as real and concrete or essential and abstract? Second, he asks whether we should think of time as homogeneous (time units are equivalent) or as heterogeneous/epochal (time units are experienced differentially); is time continuous and infinite, or atomistic and divisible? And third, he asks whether time can be measured, and if so, whether we can have more than one valid time; should time be regarded as a 'unitary quantitative commodity' or as a 'manifold qualitative experience'?[4]

It can be argued that the ways in which we answer these questions will determine how we conceptualize time. Heath's antinomies provide us with a set of basic constructs for interpreting the nature of time. Moreover, they give us tools with which not only to dissect the concept of working-time, but also with which to lay the conceptual foundations of the research perspective outlined above.[5] Indeed, these antinomies form the basis for much of the analysis which follows.[6]

Metaphor

In recent years, writers have argued that metaphor is another powerful tool for social analysis (Manning 1979; Pinder and Moore 1979; Tinker 1986). In particular, it has become popular to use metaphor (or other related tropes) when illustrating the imagery of sociological concepts (Lakoff and Johnson 1980). Morgan (1986), for example, has shown the power of metaphor for interpreting work-organizations as 'systems', 'machines', 'dramas', 'organisms', and even 'psychic prisons'.

For the concept of time, however, conceptual developments have

15

been slower (Jaques 1982, chapters 1 and 2). Thus far very few metaphors have been refined to conceptualize what is, like organization, an abstract and elusive notion. Of the few that have, the most promising to emerge have been those of the 'cycle' and the 'line'.[7]

Cyclic Time

For the metaphor of cycle, the most sophisticated of modern analyses has been that by Eliade (1959). Eliade describes how the cycle was the basic time metaphor of what he calls 'archaic' or pre-Christian man. He suggests that for archaic man, events unfolded in an ever recurring rhythm; his sense of time was developed out of his struggle with the seasons; his time horizon was defined by the 'myth of the eternal return'.[8] Eliade argues that when Christian man abandoned this bounded world for a direct, linear progression to redemption and salvation, then for the first time he found himself exposed to the dangers inherent in the historical process. Since then man has tried to master history and to bring it to a conclusion; as, for example, Marx and Hegel sought to do. Modern man seeks refuge in various forms of faith in order to rationalize a historical process that seems to have neither beginning nor end (Eliade 1959).

Linear Time

A similar argument is developed by de Grazia (1972) in his analysis of *linear* time. De Grazia suggests that, whereas primitive concepts of time are dominated by the metaphor of the cycle, for modern societies Christian beliefs give the image of time as a straight line — as a testing pathway from sin on earth, through redemption, to eternal salvation in heaven. He argues that in the evolution of modern culture the idea of irreversibility has replaced that of the eternal return. The distinguishing feature of ultimate progression led the way to a new linear concept of time; and with it a sense of firm beginning. For example, in book two of his *Confessions*, Augustine broke the circle of Roman time. In contrast to Herodotus and his notion of the cycle of human events, Augustine dispelled 'false circles' and instead purported the straight line of human history. Although

16

Anno Domini chronology became widespread only during the eighteenth century, history began to be dated from the birth of Jesus Christ (de Grazia 1972).

The Linear-Quantitative Tradition

For us, however, the linear metaphor is important because of its link with a further notion — time as a commodity. It is this link which is central to the development of a linear-quantitative tradition. During the rise of industrial capitalism this sense of uni-linearity was to find time equated with value (Thompson 1967). Technological and manufacturing innovations saw the concept become closely aligned with that of industrial progress. Time, like the individual, became a commodity of the production process, for in the crucial equation linking acceleration and accumulation, a human value could be placed upon time. Surplus value could be accrued through extracting more time from labourers than was required to produce goods having the value of their wages (Marx 1976). The emphasis was upon formality and scarcity. The images came from Newton and Descartes: time was real, uniform and all-embracing; it was a mathematical phenomenon; it could be plotted as an *abscissa*.[9]

In this tradition, industrial cultures adopt predominantly linear time perspectives. Here, the past is unrepeatable, the present is transient, and the future is infinite and exploitable (McGrath and Rotchford 1983). Time is homogeneous: it is objective, measurable, and infinitely divisible; it is related to change in the sense of motion and development; it is quantitative. Whereas in modern theology linear time has as its conclusion the promise of eternity, in the mundane, secular activities of industrialism temporal units are seen as finite. Time is a resource that has the potential to be consumed by a plethora of activities; its scarcity is seen as intensified when the number of potential claimants is increased. In advanced societies time scarcity makes events become more concentrated and segregated — special 'times' are given over for various forms of activities. Time is experienced not only as a sequence but also as a boundary condition. As functionalist sociologist Wilbert Moore states, time becomes: 'a way of locating human behaviour, a mode of fixing the action that is particularly appropriate to circumstances' (1963a: 7).

By uniting the ideas of linearity and value we begin to see time as a limited good — its scarcity enhances its worth. Lakoff and Johnson

17

(1980) crystallize this idea by citing three further metaphors to illustrate the dominant conception of linear time: time is money; time is a limited resource; time is a valuable commodity. Graham (1981), likewise, suggests that time and money are increasingly exchangeable commodities: time is one means by which money can be appropriated, in the same way as money can be used to buy time; money increases in value over time, while time can be invested now to yield money later.

This quantitative, commodified image is thus primarily a by-product of industrialism. Mumford (1934) for instance has emphasized how 'the clock, not the steam engine [was] the key machine of the industrial age' (1934: 14). He argues that rapid developments in synchronization were responsible for organizations of the industrial revolution being able to display such high levels of functional specialization. Large production-based firms required considerable segmentation of both parts (roles and positions) and activities in time and space. Such specializations set requirements for extensive time/space co-ordination at both intra- and inter-organizational levels. As high levels of co-ordination needed high levels of planning, so sophisticated temporal schedules were necessary to provide a satisfactory degree of predictability. The basis of fine prediction became that of sophisticated measurement, with efficient organization becoming synonymous with detailed temporal assessments of productivity.[10] As the machine became the focal point of work, so time schedules became the central feature of planning. During industrialism the clock was *the* instrument of co-ordination and control. The time period replaced the task as the focal unit of production (Mumford 1934).

In another landmark study, Thompson (1967) argues that industrialism sees a crucial change in the employment relation, as it was now time rather than skill or effort that was paramount. In large-scale manufacturing, the worker became subject to extremely elaborate and detailed time-discipline (Thompson 1967). Whereas prior to industrialism 'nearly all craftsmen were self employed, working in their own homes with their tools, to their own hours' (Wright 1968: 116), with the factory system came temporal rigidification. Before the industrial revolution the prime characteristic of work was its irregularity. Periods of intense working were followed by periods of relative inactivity. There was the tradition of 'St Monday', with Mondays often being taken as a casual day like Saturday and Sunday; most of the work was done in the middle of the week (Thompson 1967). Similarly, the length of the working day was irregular and determined largely by the time of the year. Thompson's quote from Hardy complements his analysis well: 'Tess . . . started her way up the dark and crooked lane or street not made for hasty progress; a street laid out before inches of land had value, and when one-handed clocks sufficiently subdivided the day' (1967: 56).

Therefore, the linear-quantitative tradition emphasises how, in contrast to the task-oriented experience of most historical and developing economies, under industrial capitalism not only have the great majority of workers become subject to rigidly deter- mined time schedules, but they have also become remunerated in terms of temporal units; that is, paid by the hour, day, week, month, or year. The omnipresence of the factory clock has brought with it the idea that one is exchanging time rather than skill: selling labour-time rather than labour.[11] Time has become a commodity to be earned, saved, or spent. Under industrial capitalism, workers are forced to sell their time by the hour (Gioscia 1972).

CLOCKTIME, CAPITAL, AND TAYLORISM

Out of this form of analysis industrial sociology has come to view modern conceptions of time as hegemonic structures whose essences are precision, control, and discipline. In industrial societies, the clock is the dominant machine of productive organization; it provides the signal for labour to commence or halt activity. Workers must consult the time- clock before they begin working. Although life in industrial societies is structured around times allocated for many different activities, it is always production that takes preference: 'Man is synchronised to work, rather than technology being synchronised to man' (de Grazia 1972: 439). Time is given to production first; other times must be fitted around the margins of the production process. Ideal organizations are those having temporal assets which are highly precise in their structuring and distribution. As technological determinism dominates our percep- tion of time, so correct arithmetical equations are seen as the solutions to time problems; there are finite limits and optimal solutions to temporal structuring. The rule is that a modern productive society is effective only if its members follow a highly patterned series of temporal conventions; each society's productive day must be launched precisely on time. In this process, clock-time holds advantages for capital as it is both visible and standardized. It has two strengths in particular: it provides a common organiz- ing framework to synchronize activities; and it commodifies labour

19

as a factor of production (Clark 1982).

It is indeed from this scenario that, for industrial sociology, Frederick W. Taylor was to emerge as the heir to Adam Smith's pin factory, and thus to become the high priest of rational time-use. It is in the manuals of industrial engineers following Taylor that were found the logical conclusions to the ideas of Smith, Ricardo and Babbage. Scientific Management, and the time and motion techniques that were its legacy, established by direct administrative authority what the machine accomplished indirectly — fine control of human actions.[12] In Taylorism we reach the highpoint in separating labour from the varied rhythms experienced in craft or agricultural work: clock rhythms replace fluctuating rhythms; machine-pacing replaces self-pacing; labour serves technology.

Thus, for industrial sociology the linear conception of time became 'commodified' due to a major change in economic development; that is, when time was discovered as a factor in production. Time was a value that could be translated into economic terms: 'it became the medium in which human activities, especially economic activities, could be stepped up to a previously unimagined rate of growth' (Nowotny 1976: 330). Time was a major symbol for the production of economic wealth. No longer was it merely sacred, given, and reproducible through the 'myth of the eternal return', but represented instead an economic object whose production is symbolized. Under industrial capitalism, timekeepers were the new regulators and controllers of work; they quantified and transformed activity into monetary value (Nowotny 1976). When time became deemed a valuable commodity then its users were obliged to display good stewardship; time was scarce and must be used rationally (Julkunnen 1977).

NEGLECT OF QUALITATIVE TIME-RECKONING

The linear-quantitative thesis is powerful because it describes how, under capitalism, time has become an object for consumption. Time is reified and given commodity status so that relative surplus value can be extracted from the labour process. The emphasis is upon time as a boundary condition of the employment relation. Time is an objective parameter rather than an experiential state.

However, the standard linear-quantitative thesis is one needing qualification. When taken up by industrial sociologists, it is often used to overstate the rationality of production practices and understate the construction of temporal meanings. There is a tendency to gloss over the fact that the industrial world is composed not simply of machine-paced work systems, but includes a wealth of work processes based on self-paced production. Temporal flexibility remains widespread in many organizational functions (e.g. sales, marketing, R and D). While, as one may expect, a good proportion of professional roles retain flexible, event-based task orientations, nevertheless many non-professional occupations operate within irregular, if not totally self-determined, work patterns (e.g. emergency services, police, maintenance crews: see Moore 1963a: 29ff). This is especially true in Britain's large service economy.[13]

Therefore, we can begin to question whether the linear-quantitative thesis should be applied so readily as the basis for explaining the nature of time at work. Whereas many writers (notably following Braverman 1974) suggest that a progressive temporal commodification accompanies increased de-skilling, other writers, although less numerous, point out that employers' time-structuring practices are far more complex, and by no means so deterministic, than much labour process theory implies (Clark 1982; Clark, Hantrais, Hassard, Linhart, and Starkey 1984; Starkey 1986; Blyton and Hassard 1988). Clark (1982), for instance, suggests that 'the claim that commodified time has to be transposed into a highly fractionated division of labour through Taylorian recipes is naive' (1982: 18). Drawing upon socio-technical theory, he offers examples of 'rational' task designs that are not anticipated by the Marxian theory of the 'porous day' (Clark et al. 1984).[14] For example, in socio-technical systems a major key to improving productivity — and also the quality of working life — is to permit temporal autonomy. Here, time structuring is taken away from the 'planners' and handed over to the 'executors'; that is, to the autonomous work group.[15]

Indeed many of the scenarios that emerge from an unrestrained linear-quantitative thesis require scrutiny. A particularly popular image is that of the rigid, standardized workday (or workweek). The standard impression of post-Taylorist work practices is of homogeneous activities being measured in micro-seconds in order to form some optimal, aggregate production output. However, as ethnographies of the production line have documented (Ditton 1979; Cavendish 1982), this image ignores the power of workgroups, on even the most externally-determined task processes, to construct their own time-reckoning systems. Whilst in comparison to other forms of organization the temporal inventories of manufacturers are exact, they remain of bounded rationality when we consider contingencies such as effort, technical failure, market demand, and withdrawals of labour. In fact, for contemporary market-based organizations, time inventories are by no means so finite and determined as the (so-called) 'rational' models would portray. Stability, and the deployment of long-term horizons are luxuries rarely available within the 'turbulent fields' of late twentieth century capitalism. Despite the emergence of technologies designed to ensure temporal stability (e.g. robotics, CAD/CAM), for the bulk of industrial production time structuring reflects the fallible judgements of planners. In practice, time systems are rarely a set of optimal solutions to mechanical problems: temporal strategies are factors which seldom equate with ideal calculations. Custom, ritual and ceremony all intrude on decision-making and the production process.[16]

It can be argued then, that working time is a much richer phenomenon than is portrayed in mainstream industrial sociology. Dominant perspectives such as functionalism and Marxian-structuralism mostly fail to capture the complexity of industrial temporality. Such paradigms concentrate either on delineating ideal-types of temporal structuring, or on suggesting that working time reflects the social relations of capitalist production. In contrast, studies of temporal experience are few. The qualitative dimension of working-time is understated, and research evidence is found only in occasional pieces of ethnography. To conduct research into the working-time, it can be argued that we need qualitative as well as quantitative approaches; we need methods which access inter-subjective features as well as structural ones — methods which describe subjective as well as objective features of time-structuring.

TOWARDS CYCLIC-QUALITATIVE TIME ANALYSIS

In developing such a qualitative approach we are not, however, as ill-equipped as we might think. The identification of qualitative themes has been a major theme in both the French and American traditions in the sociology of time. In the French tradition, the writings of Hubert (1905), Hubert and Mauss (1909), Mauss (1966), and Durkheim (1976) all emphasise the 'rhythmical' nature of social life through developing a concept of 'qualitative' time; that is, an appreciation of time far removed from writers who present it as simply measurable duration. For example, Hubert (1905) defines time as a symbolic structure representing the organization of society through its temporal rhythms, this being a theme also developed by Durkheim who analyses the social nature of time (Isambert 1979). Durkheim focuses on time as a collective phenomenon; as a product of collective consciousness (Pronovost 1986). For Durkheim, all members of a society share a common temporal consciousness; time is a social category of thought, a product of society. In Durkheim we have a macro-level exposition of the concept of social rhythm. Collective time is the sum of temporal procedures which interlock to form the cultural rhythm of a given society. Durkheim argues that: 'The rhythm of collective life dominates and encompassses the varied rhythms of all the elementary lives from which it results; consequently, the time that is expressed dominates and encompasses all particular durations' (1976: 69). For Durkheim, time is derived from social life and becomes the subject of collective representations. It is fragmented into a plethora of temporal activities which are reconstituted into an overall cultural rhythm that gives it meaning (Pronovost 1986).

In America, Sorokin and Merton (1937) also highlight this qualitative nature of social time. However, in so doing they draw not only on Durkheim, but more significantly on the works of early cultural anthropologists such as Codrington (1891), Hodson (1908), Nilsonn (1920), Best (1922) and Kroeber (1923). This synthesis allows Sorokin and Merton to identify qualitative themes at both micro and macro levels. Whilst, at the micro level, they emphasize the discontinuity, relativity and specificity of time ('social time is qualitatively differentiated', 1937: 615), they also suggest, like Durkheim, that: 'units of time are often fixed by the rhythm of collective life' (1937: 615). Indeed, they take this position a step further. Whereas Evans-Pritchard in his studies of the Nuer (1940) illustrates how certain activities give significance to social time, Sorokin and Merton adopt a position more characteristic of the sociology of knowledge. They argue that meaning comes to associate an event with its temporal setting, and that the recognition of specific periods is dependent on the degree of significance attributed to them. Drawing on Gurdon's (1914) anthropology, they argue that 'systems of time reckoning reflect the social activities of the group' (1937: 620). They show that the concept of qualitative time is important not only for primitive societies, but also for modern industrial states. They suggest that, 'Social time, is qualitative and not purely quantitative. . . . These qualities derive from the beliefs and customs

23

common to the group. . . . They serve to reveal the rhythms, pulsations, and beats of the societies in which they are found' (1937: 623).

Finally, perhaps the most ambitious attempt to outline the qualitative nature of social-time has been made by Gurvitch (1964). In a sophisticated, if at times rather opaque, thesis, Gurvitch offers a typology of eight 'times' to illustrate the temporal complexity of modern, class-bound society (i.e. enduring, deceptive, erratic, cyclical, retarded, alternating, pushing forward, explosive). He illustrates how cultures are characterized by a melange of conflicting times, and how social groups are constantly competing over a choice of 'appropriate' times. Like earlier writers, Gurvitch distinguishes between the micro-social times characteristic of groups and communities and the macro-social times characteristic of, for example, systems and institutions. He makes constant reference to a plurality of social times, and notes how in different social classes we find different of time scales and levels. He suggests that through analysing time at the societal level we can reveal a double timescale operating — with on the one hand the 'hierarchically ordered and unified' time of social structure, and on the other the 'more flexible time of the society itself' (1964: 391).

This literature suggests, then, that modern societies — as well as primitive ones — hold pluralities of qualitative time-reckoning systems, and that these are based on combinations of duration, sequence, and meaning. Unlike with homogeneous time-reckoning, there is no uniformity of pace and no quantitative divisibility or cumulation of units.[17] The emphasis is on cultural experience and sense-making: on creating temporal meanings rather than responding to temporal structures.[18] The goal is to explain the cyclical and qualitative nature of social time.

CYCLIC-QUALITATIVE RESEARCH IN THE WORK-PLACE: SOME EMPIRICAL STUDIES

On having introduced a cyclic-qualitative paradigm for work-time *thought*, we now overlay this with evidence from a cyclic-qualitative paradigm for work-time *research*. In this final section, the tone of the analysis changes, from theoretical discussion to empirical description, as we present field studies which develop this paradigm; i.e. research which yields cyclic and qualitative images of time at work. Although the paradigm is at present a nascent one, and as such there is a paucity of fieldwork to consider, we nevertheless trace four clear examples. We review Roy's (1960) account of time-structuring amongst factory workers, Ditton's (1979) analysis of the time-strategies of bakers, Cavendish's (1982) portrayal of time-battles on the assembly line, and Clark's (1978, 1982) attempts to link temporal experience with organization structure. Although these studies represent essentially isolated and unconscious attempts at paradigm building, they are important in that they move toward a nominalist ontology, produce explanations from ideographic data, and illustrate how time-structuring can be voluntarist as well as determinist. *Above all, they describe how our everyday understanding of work is based on the experience and construction of recurrent 'event-times'* (Clark 1982). As such, these cases offer examples on which to build an ethnographic, cyclic-qualitative paradigm for work-time research.

Of the above accounts, Roy's is probably the best known. In what has become a classic paper in industrial sociology, he outlines how workers who are subject to monotonous tasks make their experiences bearable by putting meaning into their (essentially meaningless) days. In Roy's machine shop, the work was both long (twelve-hour day, six-day week) and tedious (simple machine operation). He describes how he nearly quit the work immediately when first confronted with the combination of the 'extra-long workday, the infinitesimal cerebral excitement, and the extreme limitation of physical movement' (1960: 207). It was only on discovering the 'game of work' which existed within the shop that the job became bearable. The group in which he worked had established its own event-based, time-reckoning system for structuring the day — although it was one which took some time to understand. As the working day stretched out infinitely, the group punctuated it with several 'times', each of which was the signal for a particular form of social interaction. The regularity of 'peach time', 'banana time', 'window time', 'pick up time', 'fish time' and 'coke time', together with the specific themes (variations on 'kidding' themes and 'serious' themes) which accompanied each time, meant that instead of the day being endless *durée* it was transformed into a series of regular social activities. In place of one, long time horizon, the day contained several short horizons. Roy explains that after his initial discouragement with the meagreness of the situation, he gradually began to appreciate how 'interaction was there, in constant flow. It captured attention and held interest to make the long day pass. The twelve hours of "click, — move die, — click, — move die" became as easy to endure as eight hours of varied activity in the oil fields or eight hours of playing the piece work game in a machine shop. The "beast of boredom" was gentled to the harmlessness of a kitten' (1960: 215).

Ditton's analysis of the time perceptions of bakery workers is very much in the same tradition. Like Roy, he describes the social construction of times, and how workers develop 'consumatory acts to manage the monotony of time . . . breaking endless time down into digestible fragments to make it psychologically manageable' (1979: 160). He illustrates how time is both handled differently and experienced differently according to the type of work being done. For example, in the bakery there were two main production lines — the 'big (bread) plant' and the 'small (roll) plant' — each with a range of tasks. Whereas in the big plant the work was physically more difficult ('hot, hard and heavy'), it was preferred because the number and speed of events made the day pass quickly. In contrast, life on the small plant was made bearable only because slower production meant there were more opportunities to 'manipulate' time.

In the bakery study, not only do we see (as in Roy's study) the use of event-based time-reckoning to give meaning to the day, but further how such time-reckoning is strategic. Not only does Ditton show how management and workforce possess differing time strategies but, furthermore, how these are linked, directly, to their differing time orientations. Ditton distinguishes between the linear time orientation of management and the cyclic time orientation of workers. Management is consumed by the linearity of clock-time — with the calculation and division of duration, and with the unending rhythm of the machinery. Workers, on the other hand, use their knowledge of event cycles in order to control time. Indeed, the bakers possessed a whole repertoire of 'unofficial instrumental acts' for exercising control over the pace of the line, and Ditton's work is aimed, specifically, at showing how these acts were appropriated in five main ways; i.e. as strategies for 'making time', 'taking time twice', 'arresting time', 'negotiating time', and 'avoiding time'. In the bakery, individual work roles were evaluated according to their potential for manipulating time to a worker's advantage.

Cavendish (1982) is another to show the strategic importance of time in the workplace. In her account of women assembly workers 'doing time', she (even more than Ditton) portrays time as fundamental to the global struggle between capital and labour. She illustrates that as time was what the assemblers were paid for, they made sharp distinctions between 'our time and their time'. Time-obedience was the crucial discipline that management had to enforce, and skirmishes over clocking-off were more than just symbolic: 'they were real attempts by them, to encroach on our time and, by us, to resist such encroachments. . . . UMEC counted the minutes between 4.10 and 4.15 in lost UMO's, and every day the last few minutes before lunch and before the end of the afternoon were tense — each side tried to see what it could get away with' (1982: 117).

Like Roy and Ditton, Cavendish outlines how working time is not only an objective boundary condition, but also a subjective state; that is, she explains how time was experienced differently according to the social situations the work group faced. Cavendish describes how working on the line 'changed the way you experienced time altogether', and how 'the minutes and hours went very slowly but the days passed by very quickly once they were over, and the weeks rushed by' (1982: 117). She notes how there was generally a consensus amongst the women as to the speed at which time was passing: 'Everyone agreed whether the morning was fast or slow, and whether the afternoon was faster or slower than the morning' (1982: 112). She outlines how the women developed time 'rituals', and how these served both to 'make the day go faster and divide up the week'.[19] She notes how, 'All the days were the same, but we made them significant by their small dramas' (1982: 115).

However, while Cavendish, like Roy, shows how such events gave workdays some time-structure, she notes also how the phenomenological perception of time was far from homogeneous. In the interstices between rituals/events, or simply during periods when time seemed unusually burdensome, the women would devise their own, personal strategies for 'getting through' the day. Cavendish explains how: 'Sometimes 7.30 to 9.10 seemed like several days itself, and I would redivide it up by starting on my sandwiches at 8 a.m. I would look at the clock when we'd already been working for ages, and find it was still only 8.05, or, on very bad days 7.50. . . . Then I redivided the time into half hours, and ten-minute periods to get through, and worked out how many UMO's I'd have done in ten minutes, twenty minutes and half an hour' (1982: 113). Indeed, she notes how group members would adopt different strategies for getting through these periods: 'Arlene was deep in memories, and Alice sang hymns to herself. Grace always found something to laugh about, and Daphne watched everything that went on' (1982: 115). In general, Cavendish suggests that the older women were better at handling time, and that it bothered the younger women far more. In particular, the older women were more adept at 'going inside'; that is, deciding to cut-off from chatting in order to pass the time by daydreaming.

Cavendish also gives insight into how organizational-time can be reckoned differently according to the day of the working week. For example, she notes how Monday was a good day time-wise because it was the first day of the week and everyone was fresh ('it seemed a long time since Friday'), and because the group could catch up on the weekend's news. Tuesday, however, was a 'very bad day' because it wasn't special in any sense. On Wednesday the supervisor came around with the bonus points which would form part of the basis for Thursday's pay. This made Wednesday bearable; first, because the bonus points gave the group a vehicle for ritual discussion, and second because — as the points were related to the pay packet — it gave the impression that it was almost Thursday, and thus near to the end of the week ('By Wednesday lunchtime, people would say half the week was over and we could see our way to Friday afternoon'). Although Thursday was pay day, it could be experienced as a long day. This was mainly because the pay slips arrived in the first half of the morning. However, the pay slips often served as a vehicle to give the group 'a few minutes interest', especially if one of the packets had been calculated incorrectly. Friday, although being the last day of the week, was also a slow day as there we few external incidents to supplement the group's own daily rituals. Apart from the horizon of subsidized fish and chips at lunchtime, the day was a long haul to finishing at 4.10. At the end of the afternoon the women always tried to spin out the last break by an extra five minutes, so that there was then only half an hour or so to finishing time.

Finally, some of the most innovative of recent work in this area has been by Clark (1978, 1982), who in studies of two contrasting industries — sugar beet processing and hosiery manufacture — illustrates how temporal differentiation represents a crucial link between a firm's culture and its structure. Clark is one of the few writers to go beyond the small-group level and make this link.

Clark (1978) argues that in depicting organizations in a static mode, sociologists have failed to consider how structures 'vary rhythmically' (1978: 406). Following Kuznets (1933), Sorokin (1943) and Etzioni (1961), he suggests that all large firms experience periodic

28

differences in the intensity of production or service, and that these changes bring differences to the organization's character and culture.[20]

In sugar beet production Clark notes how the time frame 'contains two sharply contrasting sets of recurring activities' (1978: 12). He notes the marked differences in activities and attitudes between the period of sugar beet processing (100–20 days after 26 September) and the rest of the year (when the factory is dismantled and rebuilt by the labour force). Clark highlights the cultural rhythms that ebb and flow during the year. He illustrates the excitement at the commencement of the 'campaign' (26 September onwards); how 'start-up' is full of anticipation; and how processing seems to change the relationships between the men and their families. However, he also notes that as the campaign matures the workforce becomes somewhat alienated from the work, the corollary of this being open expressions of control by management. Indeed, by January the workforce comes to welcome the second major transitional period; i.e. when, after the processing is completed, the men are dispersed to relatively self-regulating groups with distinctive tasks. Thus, for sugar beet workers, Clark documents two distinct forms of 'temporal repertoire', with each period possessing its own normative rules and values.

In seeking a concept with which to analyse this 'structural and cultural flexibility' Clark (1982) draws upon the anthropology of Gearing (1958) and the notion of the 'structural pose'. The structural pose is a concept which denotes: the set of rules for categorizing a recurring situation; the type of social actors required for the situation; and the forms of action that should be employed. Gearing located four main structural poses in the organization of the Cherokee Indian village of the eighteenth century. He gave the example of the cue of the red flag which, although ostensibly representing the signal for conducting warfare against another village, also acted as the signal for organizing the village on a clan basis under the council of elders, and for allocating specific roles among the village community. He insists, however, that the concept does not simply imply a set of organizing procedures; for the same pose can be evoked for situations which, although of a qualitatively different nature, are deemed to require similar structural responses; as for example playing ball against another village.

For organizations, Clark uses the concept to denote how similar sequences fit several occasions. Structural poses are the tacit rules of conduct shared by those familiar with relationships between the organization's structure and culture; they are keys to anticipation and inter-subjectivity, and are founded on experience; they are blueprints which suggest the actions to take in response to certain sets of circumstances. This is well demonstrated in Clark's second field study; i.e. his account of how a marketing group within a large hosiery firm drew on its structural poses to account for, and react to, a major seasonal shift in fashion and demand. The case involved a comparison between two of the firm's marketing departments and how each handled this major shift. The two groups were from different divisions and located in different parts of the country. Further, the personnel of the departments were different, with one (Acorn) being comprised mainly of experienced staff, while the other (Harp) of staff new to the industry. Clark shows how, of these groups, only the Acorn team were able to anticipate and handle the change satisfactorily. They were able to respond to the situation by 'activat(ing) a structural arrangement by which employees in various parts of the firm were redesignated as members of an innovation group' (1982: 31). In contrast, the Harp team, who in the short four-year history of the site had only experienced seasons of expanded production, interpreted the poor sales figures as being the result, merely, of a bad season: 'It was some time before they realized that a major shift in style was unfolding. When they did realize, they had neither the credibility nor the capability to achieve the appropriate collateral structure for innovation. It was not in the structural repertoire of Harp Mill' (1982: 31).

Clark argues that organizations possess whole repertoires of structural poses based on the premise of temporal recursiveness. In developing such repertoires, employees are able to account for the recurrent, but varying, rhythms of the organization, and thus for its heterogeneous time-reckoning system. Clark's marketing study illustrates the links between temporal experience, structural differentiation and strategic time-reckoning. It indicates how organizations, over time, develop mechanisms for activating new structures from their repertoires in order to deal with anticipated events in the environment. Instead of the case turning on the linear, clock-time metaphor, it highlights the importance of cyclic, event-based trajectories.

CONCLUSIONS

In industrial sociology, the dominant image is of time as objective, measurable, highly valued, and scarce. The emphasis is upon rationality and homogeneity, and the view that time is quantifiable and evenly distributed. We accept that employment defines the pivotal time around which all other social times are structured (Pronovost 1986). As economic performance is assessed by the number of hours it takes to produce certain goods, time is given a commodity image. A corollary of this, is the portrayal of work-organizations as marvels of synchronicity; contemporary production systems, with their fine arithmetic assembly operations, are held to be the most rational of technologies; they, more than anything, epitomize quantitative time-reckoning.

However, in concentrating upon quantitative time, industrial sociologists have overlooked the importance of qualitative time. Stress has been placed on time-structuring rather than experience. The focus has been upon how time is formally patterned in task systems rather than the way it is 'made sense of' in task execution. In concentrating upon temporal structuring, and thus in treating time as a hard, objective, and homogeneous facility, we have neglected how it is experienced as a soft, subjective and heterogeneous abstraction.

Indeed, from the complex relationships linking production systems, labour, and the environment there emerge whole ranges of time patterns and rhythms. New employees learn these rhythms gradually, through experiencing how the character of work changes according to the particular time-period being endured. While most work roles are structured according to a formal inventory of activities, new recruits discover the meaning of work by reference to an informal typology of events. Tasks are categorized not only in relation to explicit work schedules, but also according to the group's own personal and social constructs (Kelly 1955). As we noted in Ditton's study, time is one of the major criteria here. The experience of work is inextricably linked to the way time is personally and socially constructed.

Therefore, in this chapter we have argued that in industrial sociology we need research which accesses not only the concrete facts of time structuring, but also the subjective essences of temporal meanings. While the discipline's conceptions of time are based, predominantly, on metaphors of linearity, rationality and quantification, we have illustrated how these images are overstated; they proffer a truncated awareness of time by ignoring the subjective and irrational features of time at work. Instead, by turning to the French and American traditions in the sociology of time, we have suggested that at the interface of sociology, philosophy, and anthropology lies a position more sensitive to temporal heterogeneity; a position capable of illuminating the cyclical and qualitative features of working time.

NOTES

1. Our aim here is to focus on social rather than physical time (Lauer 1980). The key issue is the relationship between an individual's experience and their knowledge of time, and especially in the context of work and industry.

2. Of the two major dimensions which define our existence, time and space, the former has always presented greater difficulties with regard to definition. Traditionally, the main thrust of analysis has come from philosophers, although more recently time has been a problem for physicists, biologists and historians alike. Social scientists, however, have been slower to explore the concept, with marked interest emerging only within the last fifteen years.

3. For example: 'Does time flow? Is there an arrow of time? Is time simply the perception of motion? Is there such a thing as time at all?' (Jaques 1982: xi).

4. These problematics have been given renewed potency through developments in quantum physics and relativity theory. Einstein's ideas, and others related to them (e.g. the Heisenberg principle), question the nature of relations between time, motion and change, and raise once again the issue of whether there can be more than one time.

5. It is often argued that philosophical questions such as these are merely continuing questions; that is, they do not relate to issues which can be resolved in the sense of gaining 'correct' answers. In particular, critics suggest that they are not questions which result in solutions for social problems (Friedrichs 1970). In reply to this, we argue that while they are not issues which are soluble in terms of any final logical result, they are nevertheless issues which have many pragmatic implications for the every day world of affairs (McGrath and Rotchford 1983). As a culture develops a dominant conception of time, it answers these questions at every point in its evolution.

6. As industrial sociology is displaying a greater appreciation of philosophical issues, and as its researchers are more sensitive to the assumptions which underpin their explanations, we are now able to explain concepts in ways previously foreign to us; that is, through employing a range of philosophical antinomies as a basis for analysis (see, for example, the use of nominalism-realism, positivism-anti-positivism, voluntarism-determinism, and idiography-nomothesis by Burrell and Morgan 1979).

7. Although the trend has been to contrast variations of linear and cyclical times, recently Czech sociologists Filipcova and Filipec (1986) have talked of a 'third synthetic conception' — that of spiral time.

8. This notion of the eternal return is also highlighted by Reyna (1971)

in his analysis of time concepts in Indian philosophy.

9. The 'fall into time' described by Eliade begins with the desacralization of work. Time obtains a commodity image simply because it is: 'the medium in which the results of production may accumulate' (Nowotny 1976: 331).

10. Clark (1982) illustrates how early procedures such as Wedgwood's calcuations of the 'standard costs' of labour and production (McKendrick 1962) are later transformed into mechanisms such as the extensive segmentation of internal labour markets (Edwards 1979).

11. The temporal uniformity demanded by production systems has been a major cause of industrial alienation. For example, British peasants of the eighteenth and nineteenth centuries often preferred home and poverty to the relatively well paid factory, especially when the consequence in the latter was powerlessness to change activities until dismissal time (de Grazia 1972).

12. However, the very fact that work systems are so finely paced and synchronized means that there is always considerable potential to subvert production, both through explicit and implicit forms of disruption (Cohen and Taylor 1972; Ditton 1979).

13. Although when analysing formal production systems there is a temptation to characterize all time notions as linear, several writers (e.g. Moore 1963a; Diamant 1970; and Clark 1978 and 1982) have noted the range of formal processes based on cyclic images; e.g. trade cycles and the repetition of short physical sequences (Diamant 1970).

14. Clark suggests that much labour process analysis risks the charge of being crude inductivism, especially when it insists that 'temporal inventories are highly visible and can be detected by looking for Taylorian elements' (Clark 1982: 16). Clark points out that although this assumption is widely held in the literature, it nevertheless should be challenged. Although Taylor's principles represent a tight bundle of elements — combining time study with method study, payment systems and organization structure — it is a bundle which has hardly ever been applied in its entirety in either Britain or America (see also Littler 1982).

15. Despite Clark's correction, the practice of socio-technicism has often seen capital less than willing to transfer discretion to subordinate strata (Gulowsen 1972). This is well demonstrated in Blackler and Brown's (1978) description of Volvo's experiment with a semi-autonomous dock-assembly system at the Arenal truck plant, Sweden.

16. In contemporary industrial sociology we can very much feel the impact of anthropological ideas. The current emphasis on symbolism exposes the problematic nature of assuming rationality in, for example, time-related decision-making. Myth, ritual and sentiment are all seen to intrude on decision processes.

17. Writers concerned with temporal commodification tend to treat time as absolute, whereas those who emphasize temporal heterogeneity argue for the relative nature of temporality. The latter talk of 'times' in the plural, whereas the former speak of time *per se*.

18. As noted earlier, Filipcova and Filipec (1986) suggest that we should not treat time as an exclusively linear or cyclic phenomenon, but should instead consider it as dialectical.

19. For example, at the start of the day two women visited the work station to take orders for the canteen. Some time later the same women would return with rolls and sandwiches, this prompting a ceremonial examination of the food for 'freshness, size and colour'.

20. Similarly, Moore suggests that 'it is the rhythmic recurrence of [working] patterns that permits the sense of structure' (1963a: 16).

3

Time and work:
a psychological perspective

Ken Starkey

INTRODUCTION

The concept of time is a complex one. Philosophy has taken on itself the task of answering the question, 'What is time?' Psychology's aims have been less ambitious but no less difficult, focusing not on the notion of a real, absolute time but on a more relativistic concept, the experience of time. The psychology of time has been preoccupied with how we live in time in the sense suggested by Fraisse:

> The psychological problem is no longer to know either what time is or what is the nature of our notion of time, nor is it even to seek the genesis of time in some intuition or construction of the mind: it is to understand how man reacts to situations imposed on him of living in time.
>
> (Fraisse 1964: 9–10)

The primary concern of the psychology of time is to 'study the different ways in which man adapts to the temporal conditions of his existence' (Fraisse 1964: 10). The concern is with individual and social time rather than with an ontology of time, the concern of the philosophers.

Time is a major modern preoccupation (Grossin 1974) yet it is very difficult to define precisely what time is. Many meanings have been attributed to the word 'time' but a generally accepted definition remains elusive. In this chapter a cognitive psychology concept of time as a mental construction dependent upon experience, derived from Ornstein (1969: 37), will be used. The key form of experience conditioning the experience of time is the social experience of work. Social psychologists have analysed how the experience of time is

determined by social conditions, particularly 'the rhythms and pulsations of the social life of a given group' (Sorokin 1943: 197). There
are many different ways of experiencing time and also many different
ways in which time is perceived and handled by social groups
(Zerubavel 1981: xii). Grossin (1974) has highlighted the importance
of the workgroup on the individual experience of time. The psychology
of time, therefore, needs to be a social psychology concerned primarily
with the perception and experience of time as it is affected by work.
This chapter will analyse the individual experience of time and how
this is affected by membership of an occupational group with its own
particular way of coping with the temporal demands of work. The
nature of these temporal demands affects occupational groups'
differing mental constructions concerning time.

TIME AND WORK

It is a fundamental contention of research into social time that social
life is structured and regulated at its most basic level by its temporal
parameters, that the primary determinant of the experience of time
is the experience of work (Grossin 1974) and that work provides 'the
guidelines by which adults ordinarily structure their use of time'
(Calkins 1969–70: 487). A key element of the social psychology of
time has been the stress laid on the central role of work as a determinant of temporal experience. Here it overlaps with sociological
studies which see occupation as a crucial determinant of consciousness:
'Attitudes towards everyday life . . . are extensions of habits of
thought that emerge and are developed in the practice of an occupation,
profession or craft' (Bensman and Lilienfeld 1973: 1).

Particularly important, therefore, to the experience of time is the
occupational group an individual belongs to. Occupational groups
generate their own particular attitudes to time. These attitudes help
to give an occupational group its particular character. The major
psychological study in this area is by the French social psychologist
William Grossin (1974). Grossin is concerned with 'les temps de la
vie quotidienne' ('the times of every day life') as they are created
by the experience of time generated by the individual's work situation.
Grossin argues that the experience of work is the basis for temporal
experience generally. The effects of working-time and the way in
which it is organized carry over and determine the character of
temporal experience in every day life. Different occupational groups
are characterized by different experiences of time because different

forms of work are 'more or less constraining in terms of time' (Grossin 1974: 12–13) — 'constraining' in terms of the effects they have on time in every day life. Therefore an adequate analysis of the experience of time and its determinants has to examine the interplay between individual factors (such as biographical factors like age and personality factors), individual experience, membership of an occupational group, and the work situation in particular organizations.

Time is not a scarce resource just for individuals. Organizations, too, can be, and often are, short of time. Organizations manage time scarcity in differing ways that impact on individual experience which is mediated by membership of a particular occupational group. These groups negotiate about time, seeking to impose their definitions of the best ways of organizing time on other interest groups. Views on time function as 'solidifiers of group affiliations and as mechanisms of establishing and consolidating social boundaries between groups' (Zerubavel 1979: xxi).

Traditionally, psychological approaches to time have dealt with the perception of time in terms of its pace, duration and sequencing (Cohen 1968). This chapter takes as its starting-point psychological studies of temporal structure. From these we can extrapolate constructs — dimensions of temporal experience — that are useful in understanding the experience of time at work. These dimensions are pace, length and intensity: how quickly we have to work, for how long, and the degree of fullness/emptiness that characterizes work situations. (Intensity is sometimes conceptualized in terms of 'load' — 'underload' or 'overload' — Frankenhaeuser and Gardell 1976. Work can impose too few as well as too many temporal demands.) The chapter goes on to analyse Grossin's assertion that different forms of work are characterized by different 'weights' of 'temporal constraint' and examine how different occupational groups experience their time at work, to see in what ways this temporal constraint manifests itself. A major modern manifestation of temporal constraint is a sense of being short of time. This is related to the research on occupational stress and the degree to which occupational groups differ in their experience of time scarcity. Finally the experience of time when work is not available is examined in studies of the unemployed.

THE EXPERIENCE OF TIME

Cohen, in his review of the literature on the psychology of time, talks about the difficulty of finding an adequate starting-point in any essay on time (Cohen 1968: 257). There are two reasons for this: research on time is diffuse; and, time is omni-present, a feature of all forms of experience and behaviour. Psychologists have tended to approach time in its microstructural aspects, examining what Cohen describes as 'the microstructure of subjective time', looking at how brief intervals of time are judged and compared. The lesson of these studies is that the experience of these brief intervals depends on personal, social, and cultural factors. These three sets of factors govern all our temporal experiences and the microstructural approach can be related to more common modes of experiencing and conceptualizing time and to more public forms of time-keeping. Experimental work on the psychology of the perception of time underlines the relationship between time perception, environmental conditions and mental attitudes (Fraser 1968: 585). Environmental conditions and mental attitudes, usually discussed in terms of personality characteristics, are difficult to disentangle as the two inform each other in their effect on the experience of time, be it the experience of the duration of brief time intervals or of temporal perspective (how the relationship between past, present, and future is experienced).

One of the most important psychological theories about the experience of time was put forward by Ornstein (1969). As an alternative to the concept of a biological clock as a measure of the perception of duration he suggested an information-processing approach according to which duration was related to the size of the memory store used in the encoding of information (Hanley and Morris 1982: 45). We can extrapolate from Ornstein's cognitive psychology examination of small time intervals to the experience of time in other contexts. Indeed his work is one of the most fruitful sources for theorizing about time in general. Ornstein suggests that the experience of time depends on the type of stimulus that gives rise to the experience. Time experience, therefore, differs according to the intensity of the stimulus, the number of stimuli, the associations and expectations they give rise to, and the attention we pay to the stimuli. Ornstein offers, therefore a relativistic view of time. He is concerned not with *time* but with *times*. As examples of times, he cites the time of the poet, the time of the philosopher, the times of the physicist and the biologist. All are different and if analysed individually, he argues, would generate different theories of time. His major focus is the time of the psychologist and his major concern is with the time of experiences of brief duration. This would seem to suggest a situation-specific theory of duration applicable only to the experimental psychology laboratory. His concluding remarks disclaim the generalizability of the theory of duration he has constructed when he says that theories apply only under certain conditions that need to be made explicit, and cannot account for other different experiences.

But Ornstein is being too modest. If we analyse the tasks used in his experiments we find that they do have something in common with extra-laboratory experience and the experience of time in general, namely the effect of information-content of stimuli. All stimuli, in or out of the laboratory, can be construed in terms of their information-content and their novelty effect. One of Ornstein's findings is that it takes more space to store new events (Ornstein 1969: 106). He substantiates this finding with references to experiences of ordinary life when he talks about the absence of the experience of duration and, therefore, of time for the truck driver who negotiates the same route on many occasions. Familiarity breeds automaticity of response, so the driver does not notice the passage of time. Ornstein also examines the experience of holiday time and the 'after-interval' response to the vacation experience. Whilst on the point of return but still on holiday it seems as if the holiday experience has been a long one. The novelty of holiday activity, its freshness, the comparison with the familiar routine of work, seem to lengthen the experience of holiday time while the holiday-maker is still involved in it. Yet, when the holiday is over it no longer seems at all long. 'Duration collapses' (Ornstein 1969: 111). Ornstein explains this phenomenon in terms of memory storage and the cognitive encoding process:

When we are involved in an experience one codes it complexly and notes all sorts of possible outcomes of the experience. When the experience is over (when one returns to the office) the whole (vacation) interval becomes coded, chunked over. One remembers, 'We went on vacation' instead of 'We had a fire, and went to the beach and . . .'

(Ornstein 1969: 111)

The experience of duration, then, is related to the number of events occurring within a given interval, the longer duration of the holiday period (as experienced during it) compared to the equivalent working period is explicable in terms of the greater number of novel events occurring during the holiday time. The experience of this greater novelty content expands time relative to other times.

Ornstein's work is important as a convincing critique of the sensory process approach to duration and its concept of temporal experience depending on some sort of biological clock. He demonstrated how an information-processing approach has far deeper explanatory value. His work is also important as a useful point of departure for the analysis of the everyday experience of time and for the presentation of suggestive parameters for such an analysis. Most usefully we can extrapolate from his work salient dimensions of temporal experience. The first of these is concerned with the dimension of duration: how short or how long the period of time devoted to an activity seems. The second relates to the experience of the pace of time: how quickly or slowly time passes when engaged in an activity. The third dimension relates to the content of the experience of time, its density, eventfulness, intensity. Duration, whether time feels long or short, describes extension. How full or how empty time is tells us about intensity. Ornstein's information-processing approach relates the dimensions to information content.

Fraisse (1964) has examined these dimensions and concludes that filled time has more reality than empty time. Using time-interval judgements, he found duration judged far more accurately if the interval involved a greater density/intensity of activity. Durations filled by sound tended to be over-estimated, empty durations, soundless intervals between two sounds were greatly under-estimated. In extra-laboratory situations the experience tends to the opposite. Filled time passes quickest, empty time drags on and on. The effect of attention, though, is constant in both situations on the length of the time experience: 'The greater the attention the longer the interval seems' (Fraisse 1964: 147). Fraisse also points to the importance of attitude to the experience of time when he implies that we tend to make comparisons between the times we experience and the times we would ideally like to experience: 'Feelings of length of time can arise during the duration itself through a comparison between the duration we feel and the duration we should like' (Fraisse 1964: 232). The ideal can serve as a touchstone for the judgement of the other dimensions of temporal experience too.

We have isolated three dimensions according to which the experience of time can be categorized and judged: duration, pace and intensity. It has been implied that the dimensions can most usefully be conceptualized as bi-polar: long-short, fast-slow, and full-empty. On these dimensions there are positions which we experience as more satisfying than others. Also, the dimensions interact and are, thus, somewhat difficult to isolate. Duration experiments have shown how equivalent time intervals can pass more or less quickly, intervals can seem long or short, if judged separately, or longer or shorter if compared. According to Bachelard we notice length of time only when we find it too long (Bachelard 1950). Or, expressed differently, we find pace of time only when we find it too slow, though when we put it this way we see that the statement is only a half-truth. We also find length of time and pace of time when we find it too short or that it passes too quickly. Intensity relates to extensity as, for example, in the difference between the times of the old and young. Time passes more quickly for the old than the young. Fraisse (1964) explains this in terms of the novelty content of the stimuli they are exposed to. To the young everything is new and to be freshly experienced and savoured. The old have seen it all before and repeated events do not have the same intensity of impact. Harton (1939) looked at the effect of the experience of success and failure on the experience of time and found that success was associated with a quicker passing of time than a failure experience of equivalent duration.

Lynch (1972) has tried to disentangle the links between the dimensions and their linguistic description. In a study of the central business district of Chicago he found that respondents could answer unequivocally when asked when they found time passing 'fastest' but the concept of time passing 'slowest' was ambiguous. 'Slow' could mean either 'pleasantly calm or leisurely' or 'when time drags' as, for example, when waiting impatiently or when performing unpleasant work. Slowness here involves both the dimensions of pace and intensity. Its first usage implies that the time is experienced with an optimal degree of fullness, the second that it is not full enough. The experience of time can, therefore, be judged in terms of whether it is too full or too empty, just as it can be judged as too long or too short, too fast or too slow. On each of these dimensions there is an optimum point of experience, described by Csikzentmihalyi (1975) as 'flow' when all dimensions are in balance, which he discerns in both work and play, in the activity of the surgeon, the musician and the rock-climber, among others, when involved totally in their tasks.

What has been said so far cuts across two ways of looking at time that have been explored by philosophers. The dominant modern view of time is to regard it as a homogeneous variable. This view, important as it is, does not do justice to our experience of time, which is 'basically one of continuous repetition in a rhythmic form rather than of linear homogeneity' (Orme, 1969: 66). A homogeneous conception of time has been fundamental to modern western man's methods of conceptualizing time, which is viewed in terms of extension in space. The clock, the prime exemplar of this mode of conceptualizing, measures time by movement of its parts through two-dimensional space. Philosophers, such as Bergson, have argued that this constitutes

41

a radical limitation of our ability actually to understand the temporality of our experience. The alternative view of time sees it in terms of depth. The contrast is between quantitative time — continuous, homogeneous and, therefore, measurable because equal parts are equivalent: and qualitative time — heterogeneous, discontinuous, and unequivalent when different time periods are compared (Hubert and Mauss 1909). Time can be construed, then, as something that can be isolated if its boundaries are specified or as a flow of events (Moore 1963a: 17). Duration, the measure of time allocated to activity, does not, as Moore puts it elsewhere, demonstrate the intensity, the depth of the experience (Moore 1963b: 165).

Kern, in his historical analysis of modes of thinking about time, sees the period from around 1880 to the beginning of the First World War as a watershed in the evolution of our ability to understand time. A one-dimensional perspective based on a homogeneous, atomistic conception of time was no longer adequate to withstand the critique of a relativistic mode of thinking about time which emphasized its heterogeneity (Kern 1983: 16). Kern seems to imply that the relativistic mode replaced its predecessor. It is rather the case that it radically altered the possibilities for thinking about time but that the two modes then had to co-exist, if somewhat uneasily. It is debatable how deeply the relativistic mode has bitten into consciousness. Indeed, some of the phenomena Kern discusses, such as the management of time during the First World War, represent a tightening-up of the homogeneous view. What we have inherited is an attempt to theorize about time as an uneasy relationship between the two modes.

Kern shows that one of the major breakthroughs of the period he writes about was the demonstration of 'the reality of private time' and that 'Bergson's philosophy forms the theoretical core of the argument for private time' (Kern 1983: 8). For Bergson, time is the fundamental aspect of consciousness. He attacked the atomistic view of time that stemmed from Newton's calculus, in which time was no more than the sum of infinitesimally small but discrete units and argued that time is actually a flux (*durée*), irreducible to a sum of component parts. In this he was supported by the view of consciousness as a stream, as opposed to the summation of discrete units, put forward by William James in the same period. Experience is, therefore, a continuity, a flowing, a form of becoming, and time is its fundamental aspect. The plurality of experiences of time in its heterogeneous and fluid forms was also explored in the literature of the period, by Mann, Proust, and Joyce, for example, as well as by the philosophers. They shared with Bergson the exploration of consciousness as an 'active tension' of different *durées* (Kern 1983: 32). Social scientists later applied the idea to the analysis of social existence. Sorokin compares two lives of the same quantitative duration but of very different qualitative durations (*durées*). 'One life career may be filled mainly with an empty ''killing'' of time, the other may be packed with human experience' (Sorokin 1943: 209). Time measured by clocks and calendars is incommensurate with duration, pace, or intensity.

Bergson (1910) emphasizes this point when he argues that subjective time can speed up and slow down. Bergson also argued that what science had traditionally called time — a tradition that Einstein was soon to disrupt — was not duration but its spatialization, because only by conceptualizing it in spatial terms does time become measurable, divisible, and homogeneous. For Bergson this implied a reduction of reality, the triumph of quantity over quality (Bergson 1910: 97). Philosophers such as Kant have made the same mistake of seeing time as homogeneous (Minkowski 1970: 18). Bergson critiques the 'mistaken idea of a homogeneous inner duration, similar to space, the moments of which are identical and follow, without penetrating, one another' (Bergson 1910: 109). Bergson highlights the importance of a qualitative, relativistic approach to time and the importance of the dimensions of pace, duration, and intensity. Reflective consciousness, according to Bergson, has to free itself from 'the ghost of space', which is all that remains of the experience of time when it is 'conceived under the form of an unbounded and homogeneous medium' (Bergson 1910: 99).

Psychology has to free itself from space if it wants to understand time in terms of pace, intensity, and duration and, thus, apprehend 'the ceaselessly flowing current of time, which represents the flux of reality' (Glasser 1972: 293). This means the analysis of the experience of time as 'an alternation of fullness and emptiness, of action and rest' (Fraisse 1964: 78).

TIME AND WORK

Industrial progress brought a new managerial time-discipline, an intensification of working time which rendered it 'denser, heavier, more tiring' (Grossin 1969: 163–4). Work organization came to depend increasingly upon a highly rational, structured, formal, and quantitative aproach to time (Gunnell 1970: 82). Time-keeping led to time-accounting, time-rationing, and abstract time (Mumford 1973). Grossin (1974) sees rigidity as the dominant characteristic of modern work. Previously time was subordinated to task. Now this relationship is reversed. Modern work typically involves:

> Rigidity, precision, compartmentalization of the time structures of work . . . . [Work] activities are firmly fixed in pre-prepared pigeon-holes that have to be filled. Industry thus separates time and task. Time assigns task. Arriving at work, the worker has in front of him a prepared network of measured times and . . . repetitive tasks. These make up separate equal periods according to which he assigns his movements without any choice in the matter.
> (Grossin 1974: 376)

The evolution of managerial controls leads to an increase in the pace and intensity of work as its length is reduced and there is an increasing sense of temporal constraint in the experience of time at work.

Grossin's arguments concerning temporal constraint are corroborated by the sociologists of time (Hassard, this volume) who highlight the crucial significance of a commodified approach to time to the way work is organized. Time is a key factor of work organization. Organizations survive as 'practices which are deeply sedimented in time-space' (Giddens 1979: 80). Organizations depend upon the synchronization of activity, its correct sequencing and an agreed rate of work (Moore 1963b: 163). Organizational survival depends upon the ability to organize the routine. Individual socialization into an organization is comprised in large part of adaptation to the demands of organizational time: 'Little can be accomplished . . . of organizational interest unless [the newcomer] can locate himself along the . . . axes of organizational time and space' (van Maanen and Katz 1979: 33).

Just as time is limited as a personal resource (Becker 1977), organizations usually operate under conditions of time scarcity (Hill, this volume; Blyton, this volume). Time-use, therefore, has to be maximized using the clock as the touchstone of time-management. The commodification of time, the measuring of time like any other commodity, facilitates the measurement and the comparison of different ways of organizing time. However, the more time is commodified and the more work is subjected to the dictates of clock-time, the more the experience of time at work — in terms of the dimensions of pace, duration, and intensity — becomes oppressive. Our whole culture is geared to the avoidance of loss of time (Soule 1956). Social life has come to be characterized by a chronic shortage of time (Linder 1970).

Given this condition of scarcity, time has to be 'planned, allocated, clipped, saved, and spent' according to a system of priorities, the main, and often the exclusive one of which is economic (Calkins 1969–70: 487). As a result contemporary life is indelibly marked by an economic orientation to time use which, of necessity, commodifies time and makes maximization of its usage a psychological as well as social necessity (Linder 1970). The logic of industrial development entailed concomitant changes in temporal experience. The shift to an industrial economy created a radical change in temporal perspective from that dominant in an agricultural society; as the scale of industrial organization developed, so did pressure towards synchronization and co-ordination of the punctuality and regularity of activity. Kern points out that during the period he studied at the turn of this century there was a change of attention towards short intervals of time. For the first time these became important in such forms as time-limited interviews, brief telephone conversations, transient meetings (Kern 1983: 110–11). Mental life was increasingly marked by acceleration of its pace (Simmel 1903). According to Lukacs (1971), time lost its qualitative character. The general pace of life increased, a phenomenon predicted by economists of time (Soule 1956, Linder 1970, Becker 1977). The clock also made possible the development of the schedule, the tendency of which, according to economic rationale, is to become increasingly durationally rigid (Zerubavel 1981).

There is, therefore, as a result of these developments, a process of increasing temporal constraint. Chronarchy, the rule of time, results in the extensive control of time (Wright 1968). This has its corollary in tightening schedules, a constant search for increased speed (Moore 1963a), and an 'obsession with marked time' (Cohen and Taylor 1972). Co-ordination goes hand in glove with acceleration. In contrast, a time-surplus primitive culture like the Nuer's cannot experience the feeling these trends engender of fighting against time (Evans-Pritchard 1940: 103). Chronarchy leads to forms of work organization and time co-ordination that tend towards rigidity, precision, punctuality, calculability, standardization, bureaucratization, invariance, and routineness (Zerubavel 1981). Emphasis on the maximization of time-use leads to an increase in the pace of work. This is very significant for the experience of time at work, because pace is 'probably the most insistent, the most basic aspect, of a job' (Blauner 1964: 28). Assembly-line work, particularly in the motor industry, has typically been seen as a prototype of industrial work under capitalism and studies have painted a picture of its time as homogeneous and unremittingly oppressive (Blauner 1964). On the line, speed is all — the assembly line was the perfect solution to problems of economies of speed (Chandler 1977: 281) — so this form of work is seen as totally dictated in its every move by the clock (Wright 1968: 208). The synchronization and co-ordination, the regularization of continuous output, are management's most important criteria. The line controls the pace of work and dictates every movement. The work cycle is very short and the work soon becomes boring, mechanical and repetitive (Braverman 1974: 32). The line's chief advantage from management's point of view is that it makes possible a set rate of work and, thus, the control of time by imposing a set speed of working. Its introduction 'resolved technologically the essential first control task: it provided unambiguous direction as to what operation each worker was to perform next' (Edwards 1979: 188). Job redesign and work humanization have led to an emphasis on jobs with longer work cycles. They have therefore become less fragmented and granted more autonomy to the production worker in allocating time, even on the car assembly-line (Starkey and McKinlay 1988).

The experience of time at work has been analysed most thoroughly by the French social psychologist, William Grossin (1974). According to Grossin, different occupational groups are characterized by different experiences of time, because different forms of work are 'more or less constraining in terms of time' (Grossin 1974: 12–13) constraining in terms of the general effect they have on time in everyday life. There is a gradient of constraint. Grossin contrasts industrial, office, peasant, and professional work. In these forms of work the gradient stretches from teaching (least constraining) to industrial piece-work (most constraining). Time at work is more or less constrained by the way particular forms of work are organized. Different groups of workers differ in their ability to create their own forms of time according to the degree of time-discipline their work imposes on them. A dominant feature of modern temporal experience, Grossin argues, is that it is clock-bound, regulated according to the mechanical time of the clock. He relates this to dysfunctional consequences of work for workers who are ruled by the clock, most notably their sense of alienation from their work. The clock disrupts the relationship between task and time. By having tasks timed, workers are faced with a constant struggle against time so that it is the clock and abstract, mechanical time not the nature of the task itself that determines how much time workers should devote to a task. Modern workers compared to their pre-industrial predecessors are no longer free to adapt their working time to the demands of the work task as they best see fit. Rather, they have to conform to the demands of the clock. There is, consequently, a caesura between human time and industrial time. The resultant alienation is manifested in attitudes to and ways of experiencing time in every day life. The constraining effects of worktime impact on life away from work.

Grossin emphasizes the aspects of excessive pace and rigidity when he discusses industrial work. But not all work imposes the same homogeneous form of time. As Grossin (1974) demonstrates, different kinds of work give rise to different experiences of time. For example, craft industries retain their own unique work rhythm, based on the somewhat unpredictable time requirements of particular tasks. Continuous-process technologies create a new rhythm which some authors, most notably Blauner (1964), see as liberating in terms of its time demands. This work is characterized, according to this view, by a long period of calm, involving primarily the monitoring of the smooth running of the process, and infrequent periods of crisis. This generates what Blauner terms a 'calm and crisis' mode of time experience. His views of the liberating, non-alienating potential of work in these high-technology industrial environments has been criticized. Writers such as Gallie have argued that the 'calm and crisis' time experience is not a general one and that it applies to only a very small section of the workforce in industries using this technology (Gallie 1978: 296).

For Grossin it is the clock that is the key determinant of the experience of temporal constraint. The more work is organized according to the clock, the more constraining it is (Grossin 1969: 134–5). But not all work suffers to the same extent from domination by the clock. Grossin contrasts industrial and professional work. Industrial work, manual and unskilled or semi-skilled, is of diminishing centrality as a representative mode of work situation as the numbers employed in manufacturing dwindle and work in the service sector comes to predominate. The industrial worker suffers from the greatest degree of temporal constraint. The office worker has more temporal autonomy even if still greatly constrained by routine. The peasant — Grossin looks at the work situation of the vineyard worker — is least constrained by the clock. Such work still depends on the rhythms of nature, so peasants have a positive relationship to time, not seeing it as an enemy to be struggled against. The professional — Grossin looks at the work of the teacher — has a more complex relationship to time than the other occupational groups. Teachers' experience of working-time is more various, part of their time being characterized by the rigid demands of the school timetable, the rest of the working-time being under their own control. But even within the constraints of the timetable, teachers' time manifests much variety, as no two lessons are exactly the same (Grossin 1974: 117). Professionals, like peasants, have a positive relationship to time. '[They do] not experience the weight of immediate temporal constraint like those workers bound by piecework or the speed of the line' (Grossin 1969: 69).

Writers on professional work have argued that, relative to other forms of work in industrial society, this kind of work has escaped submission to the dictates of clock-time. It is organized according to a sequence of tasks rather than a formal timetable based on hours of work (Lamour and de Chalendar, 1974: 108). Moore (1963a) argues that professional work tends to be task- rather than time-orientated. Grossin associates professional work with high degrees of temporal freedom, an association the professional ideology of work supports. Professionals argue that only they are capable of organizing their own time to best effect because only they understand the complex nature of their work. They, therefore, resist management attempts to subvert what they construe as a right to self-management of their time (Starkey 1986). Their work, they maintain, is non-routine, unprogrammed and unprogrammable, and, because of this task-orientation, cannot be 'precisely time-oriented' (Moore 1963b: 162):

> The determination of precise man-hour requirements . . . is most subject to discretion for those farthest from the production processes. [Also] the need for temporal co-ordination like specificity of man-hour requirements tends to decrease with structural distance from machine processes.
>
> (Moore 1963b: 166–7)

Professionals retain a task-orientation to work because the kind of problems they deal with 'have a way of being temporally undisciplined' (Moore 1963a: 29). Autonomy and independence suggest freedom to control time as the professional deems fit. Time-discipline, therefore, is much less apparent in professional work than in lower status occupations, where work is organized according to rigid temporal formats based on the clock (Grossin 1974: 380).

Grossin bases his claims for the temporal advantage of professional groups on his study of French teachers. It is illuminating to compare the English teacher's time situation with that of the French teacher as described by Grossin. A superficial comparison of English and French teachers demonstrates the more privileged position of the

the French. As with German teachers (Dunham 1980), they are less burdened with extra-academic roles such as supervision and control of pupils outside the classroom. The French have a system of *surveillance* in which non-academic staff, responsible for discipline, deal with these matters, leaving teachers to concentrate on their academic role. Also French teachers possess higher social status, the better qualified ones anyway. Grossin comments on their relative satisfaction with their salaries. Their English counterparts would hardly concur. The French teacher is satisfied with time rather than money, going as far as reversing the old adage 'time is money' in favour of time. As they have enough money, time becomes more important than more money.

In Grossin's study only 23 per cent of the French teachers agreed that 'time is money', 12 per cent were undecided and 65 per cent disagreed. In a questionnaire study of a sample of British teachers (Starkey 1986), 32.6 per cent agreed that 'time is money', 21.7 per cent were undecided and only 45 per cent disagreed. French teachers seem less obsessed with time as far as this can be judged by their reliance on their watches: 35 per cent consulted their watch very often and 50 per cent rarely, while among English teachers 78 per cent attached great importance to their watch and only 13 per cent little importance. In response to a choice between time and money, extra work hours for extra wages, fewer hours and lower wages, and no alteration to the present situation, French teachers were mostly happy with their lot: 73 per cent did not want to alter their present situation, 24 per cent wanted to work less for lower wages, while only three per cent wanted to work more for higher wages; 51 per cent of the English sample wanted no change; 11 per cent wanted to work less for lower wages, while 38 per cent wanted to work more and earn more.

These findings are suggestive of strong differences in attitudes to time between French and English teachers. English teachers are more concerned with improving their financial situation, the French seem satisfied with theirs. English teachers seem more concerned with clock-time, indicative of more pressure on them in this respect. Dunham's study suggests that the situation of English teachers is more prone to stress generally than that of their continental counterparts. In France a higher level of education tends to correlate with the tendency 'to liberate oneself from too tight temporal constraints' (Grossin 1974: 163). English teachers as a professional group have not yet gained this privilege unambiguously.

The position of professional groups is not, therefore, as unambiguous as Grossin suggests. Professionals, to the degree they become members of bureaucratic organizations and are subjected to their rules and regulations, lose temporal autonomy (Starkey 1988a). Indeed, it has been suggested that:

> One of the most significant aspects of the rationalization of social life in modern Western civilization is the increasing bureaucratization of professional commitments, which is clearly manifested through the rigidification of their temporal boundaries.
>
> (Zerubavel 1981: 159)

Current efforts by the state to make professional groups more accountable for their services and, thus, more efficient, have emphasized the importance of an adequate return on time and the importance of a rational allocation of time to professional tasks (Starkey 1986).

No occupational group's temporal position is static. Job redesign has altered the temporal aspects of work on the assembly-line, giving production workers enhanced choice over the way their working time is organized (Robertson and Smith 1985). Skilled groups of workers are subjected to increasing time-discipline. Railway drivers recently fought a hard and ultimately unsuccessful struggle to retain the eight-hour day as the basis of the organization of their working time, arguing that the flexible rostering — the British Rail Board's replacement for the eight-hour day — would create intolerable levels of stress and disruption to family life in a job that was already, because of its time demands, highly stressful (Starkey 1988b).

TIME AND OCCUPATIONAL STRESS

The example of the resistance of railway drivers to new shift arrangements demonstrates the link between time and occupational stress. Railway drivers objected to the stress new shift rosters would generate. Time plays an important if under-examined role in the stress experience. Grossin talks about the pathological effects of 'temps trop durs' (times that are too hard). Social-psychological studies of stress have concentrated on such factors as life-events (Gundersen and Rahe 1974) and personality factors (Friedman and Rosenman 1974). Time as a potential stressor is a recurring factor in these studies. In life-events studies it is the accumulation of stressful events in time, their rapid succession, that takes individuals beyond their limits of coping. Type-A behaviour is characterized by time-urgency. Individual stress at work is a complex interaction of occupational stressors — such as time pressures, role overload, role ambiguity and role conflict (Cooper and Marshall 1976) — and individual personality factors. A primary potential time stressor is temporal constraint, which is often manifested in excessive pace of duration of work. For Grossin temporal pressure has two facets — speed and task overload, i.e. a shortage of time to accomplish work tasks. Time stress, therefore, arises when time is too fast or too full.

Paradoxically, professionals seem most prone to stress related to the experience of time at work. The paradox occurs because stress is related to the temporal advantage professionals enjoy in comparison with other groups of workers. Grossin makes the point that whatever temporal advantages accrue to managers over their subordinates relate to the content of the worktime and the managers' relative freedom to organize this as they see fit, rather than to the extent of time on the job. Advantage arises in its substance and not its geometry, the ability to control how to use time not in the length of time devoted to work (Grossin 1969: 69). Professionals, imbued with the ideology of work, tend to work long hours as work provides a central life-interest (Anthony 1977). Professionalism encourages systematic over-work (Medawar 1982: 150). It is professionals who tend to manifest type-A personalities characterized by over-involvement in work, high achievement orientation, a sense of being overworked and of the urgency of time (French et al 1982: 18).

Because their days are not tightly disciplined by a work timetable and because their time is at their own discretion, professionals tend to lose control of their time if control of time is construed as being able to devote time to anything but work: 'Ever-availability [is a] symbolic expression of being professionally committed' (Zerubavel 1981: 153). Instead of being in control of time professionals have been described as 'slaves to the system' (Pahl and Pahl 1971: 259). That they are willing does not alter the fact that the element of choice has been undermined, thus creating the element of slavery. Pahl and Pahl argue that managers' time is more effectively exploited than the time of the men they manage because they have 'internalized an ideology of self-coercion' (Pahl and Pahl 1971: 259). This assertion is corroborated by Anthony (1977) in his study of commitment to work.

Managers' control over their own working time is limited. Studies of managers have shown how much they are at the beck and call of others, reacting rather than acting in a proactive manner, and how their time is fragmented and their activities episodic (Pugh et al 1975,

Mintzberg 1973). The popularity of time-management courses for managers is based on the ill-founded assumption that time is a commodity that is amenable to a highly prescriptive programme of analysis and self-help activity. The prevalence of managerial stress points to the over-simplification of this approach.

Members of the helping professions are particularly prone to occupational stress and 'burn-out', a key factor in which is the long and intense hours they work (Carroll 1979, Gerber 1983). Amongst professionals stress tends to occur because of overload. In other forms of work, occupational stress is more likely to arise because of underload. Frankenhaeuser and Gardell (1976) studied workers on a moving belt in a sawmill. Those working on the belt suffered high levels of stress because of the demand the work made on them to:

> Make skilled and economically important decisions in an extremely short time, at a pace completely set by the machine system. . . . The production system consistently forces the worker to perform below his standards. He is constantly aware that the quality of his work is lower than it 'ought' to be. He is simply not allowed the time to do a good job. Thus, the work is not only characterized by quantitative overload but also by qualitative underload, owing to the fact that the worker's skill is constantly underutilized.
>
> (Frankenhaeuser and Gardell 1976: 443)

The authors conclude that the monotony and coercion of the job could be improved:

> By increasing individual control over the pace and rhythm of the work, and by allowing workers more freedom in deciding how to allocate their personal resources in the course of work.
>
> (Frankenhaeuser and Gardell 1976: 41–2)

Worktime, then, can become a stressor when it is either too dense or not dense enough. Optimal time demands occur between these two extremes (Csikzentmihalyi 1975). Workers generally strive to avoid the stress of empty time, creating their own rituals to fill time if not enough work is available (Roy 1960). Roth's study of the importance of timetables (Roth 1963) also demonstrates the psychological importance of temporal structure (see next section). Moore, in an examination of automated process industry work, found, contrary to Blauner, that time was viewed negatively because much of the work involved waiting around for something to happen. This was experienced as doing nothing and was not enjoyed by the workforce because of the lack of any routine with which to structure time (Moore 1963a). Nowhere is the need for adequate temporal structure more apparent than in the studies of the effects of unemployment, to which we turn our attention next.

TIME OUT OF WORK

A dominant feature of western industrial society is time scarcity. Other 'primitive' cultures are characterized by a surplus of time (Evans-Pritchard 1940, Bohannon 1953). In our culture only the unemployed or the under-employed experience such a surplus, and that usually unwillingly, often with disintegrative personality effects. Studies of the unemployed demonstrate that they tend to deteriorate psychologically under the weight of empty time. One effect of this deterioration is a diminishing ability to structure time (Jahoda *et al* 1972, Jahoda 1979, Starkey and Walsgrove 1985). The temporally dysfunctional effects of unemployment are particularly apparent in the long-term unemployed. The classic study of Marienthal (Jahoda *et al* 1972) demonstrates the anomic consequences unemployment has in individuals' daily lives. The loss of work, and the rhythmic quality work gives to social life, impairs the time sense. Amongst the unemployed the watch loses its function of organizing device, unpunctuality becomes the rule, plans for the future become more and more difficult to make, the individual becomes trapped in an endless present. Jahoda's update of the earlier study supports these findings (Jahoda 1979) and demonstrates the need for a certain amount of temporal structure as well as the crucial function of work in providing this structure.

Work offers a basic structure for the every day use of time. Having too much time on one's hands is associated with greater life dissatisfaction than having too little. Greater life satisfaction is generally associated with a scarcity rather than a surplus of free time (Robinson 1977). In its absence the constraint of the clock is ardently desired because a key function of the clock is to order time. Temporal problems similar to those experienced by the unemployed arise in organizations characterized by time surplus. Calkins (1969–70) looked at the problems individuals experience in structuring their time in one such a setting, a medical institution with long-term residents. The major time problem she addresses is the problem of 'getting lost in time' due to the lack of structure in day-to-day activity. The main fear of the residents was of 'drifting' in time, losing touch with it as a definite feature of their lives and, thus, losing contact with reality. Temporal pressure may be constricting and constraining, but it is also 'the framework within which our personality is organized. When it is absent we are disorientated. There is nothing to bind the sequence of our activities; we are alone' (Fraisse 1964: 289–90).

Fraisse concludes that the human psyche is too precarious to cope without fixed positions in space and regular cues in time. The psychopathology of time shows what happens when this precarious equilibrium is interrupted (Minkowski 1970). Psychopathology disrupts the time-sense, just as unemployment or extended illness does. A major consequence of these is the disruption of time perspective, the way we relate to past, present and future and integrate our behaviour to include these. For western man, the relationship to the future is particularly important: 'Man's feeling tone is determined less by his present activities than by his future-time perspective. Western man [is] a creature governed by hopes and anxieties' (Farber 1953: 256). A future time-orientation dominates over present-centredness. The present is tolerable only if there is hope for the future. Psychopathology or unemployment disrupt the relationship to the future, which is an intrinsic element of 'the right relationship to time' (Bollnow 1977).

A classic study of the problems of structuring time in organizations that do not provide sufficient temporal cues is Roth's (1963) examination of individuals who are forced to leave the work situation due to a long period of hospitalization. They take to their hospital environment time norms generated by work expectations, norms concerning the predictability of their trajectories through time which are inapplicable to the uncertainty of their temporal prospects. Roth's main focus is on tuberculosis patients although he extrapolates from this group to others. The time problems associated with this disease arise (or arose in the 1960s) from the prognostic uncertainties. The course of the disease is notoriously difficult to predict. Barthes' description of tuberculosis captures its temporal ambiguities: 'disease without pain or consistency . . . with no other signs than its interminable time and the social taboo of contagion' (Barthes 1975: 39).

To overcome the uncertainty arising from the unpredictability about how long cure will take, and treatment, and hospitalization, will last — an uncertainty medical staff are unable to allay and find difficult to manage — patients resort to their own methods of managing time. They create their own timetables based on a variety of what they take to be prognostic indicators, most notably the experience of their peer group, other patients suffering from the same disease. These timetables serve to diminish uncertainty and, although they provide false hope in those cases that do not conform to the timetable, they do, generally, make the period of hospitalization seem less endless as they split the large blocks of time that would otherwise exist, without any clear markers or transition points from one stage of the illness to the next in the process of healing, into smaller manageable units (Roth 1963: 12). These self-generated timetables with their norms of speed of progress and markers based on key events on the road to recovery offer patients a means of structuring their time. Dissonance arises when patients' timetables and their doctors' medical timetables clash because patients 'maintain a constant pressure to be moved along faster'.

Roth sees similar acts of timetable creation in other situations where explicit time norms are not available and time is not structured in an obvious, predictable manner. He examines this in other medical settings, such as psychiatric treatment units and in polio convalescence, and also in work settings. Similar problems of structuring time arise at work concerning career progress, when the organization does not provide clear cues about how a person should expect to progress through a career or when an individual feels he or she has fallen behind what he/she construes as group norms for career progress. Roth argues that the structuring of the passage of time by establishing a timetable based on informal norms is an inevitable reaction when an organization does not provide the individual, or the group, with a formal, established pattern: 'People will not accept uncertainty. They will make an effort to structure it no matter how poor the materials they have to work with' (Roth 1963: 93). They will structure the passage of time by creating benchmarks or reference points (Davis 1963).

CONCLUSION

A key factor in psychological wellbeing is an adequate sense of temporal structure. Time problems arise when there is too much or too little structure. The key factor in the experience of time from a social-psychological perspective is membership of an occupational group. Submission to time might constitute 'the price of modernization, productivity [and] potential affluence (Landes 1983: 360) as industrial society advances and the clock becomes increasingly dominant; but, as Grossin (1974) points out, the degree of submission to the clock and experience of time varies according to form of work.

There is a heterogeneity of work situations, differing in their degree of temporal constraint. Workers' experiences of time differ in pace, duration, and intensity. Work displays both positive and negative temporal features. On the positive side it serves as a basic temporal structuring device. On the negative side it can impose too much structure. Time is a key factor in the genesis of occupational stress. Time demands can cause stress when they are too many (overload) or too few (underload). The most temporally disadvantaged are those without work, where underload is greatest and the need for temporal structure, in its absence, most evident.

Finally we must not forget the individual and the choice he or she makes concerning the occupational role bargain — the degree of commitment he or she makes to the work role. How time at work is ultimately experienced will depend on degree of commitment. The key factor is the degree to which the time structure demanded/offered by membership of a particular occupational group is embraced by the individual: 'Human resources of energy and time are flexible. They expand and contract, depending upon very particular systems of commitment that determine availability' (Marks 1977: 935). Energy is the ability to do work (Miller 1977). Time becomes scarcer at work to the degree that commitment to occupation increases:

> Time does not present itself to us as prefabricated scarcity even in modern settings. Like energy it is flexible, waxing abundant or scarce, slow or fast, expanded or contracted, depending upon particular socio-cultural and personal circumstances. . . . We need to see the experience of both time and energy as outcomes or productions of our role bargains, rather than assuming . . . that they are already constituted for us as scarcities even before our role bargains are made. (Marks 1977: 929)

The individual has to come to terms with his/her occupational role and decide the degree to which he/she will embrace it.

4

Time at work: an economic analysis

Stephen Hill

INTRODUCTION

Time in economics is generally perceived as either a calibration of change, allowing variations in economic values to be measured, or as some scarce resource in the production and consumption decisions of individuals and organizations. Time is treated as an independent variable in forecasting models, and as the justification for interest payments in the analysis of investment (i.e. interest as the reward for waiting). Time as a social or psychological concept has had little significance in the development of economics, in which time, if mentioned at all, has been usually calendar. As Sharp points out:

> There is no particular economic reason why interest should be paid, or dividends declared every time the earth completes one circuit around the sun . . . but the earth calendar has been built into economic calculations. (Sharp 1981: 8)

However one area in which calendar time has been avoided is in the treatment of change (economic dynamics). Economists distinguish between the short and long run as time periods, defined in terms of partial or full adjustment to a change in some economic variable. Thus, for example, price elasticity will be lower in the long run as supply adjusts to a change in price. Even this distinction becomes blurred in practice, depending on the adopted definition of partiality.

It is in the analysis of time at work that duration has been made most explicit. The simplest economic models describe a trade-off between working-time (and income generated) and leisure time. Here leisure time is not defined in terms of the calendar or activities, but simply as time not at work. Then leisure time and income both generate satisfaction, whilst worktime is the price paid for such satisfaction. As later sections will show, this dichotomy has now been superseded by the recognition that working time may generate utility and that some of what was previously regarded as leisure time may be used productively.

This chapter will not attempt a full description or analysis of time at work in its many dimensions. Rather it will concentrate on the essence of the individual choice model and its development, leaving the philosophy underlying the economic concept of time and the extensions of the working time model to the writings of others (useful starting points for intended readers would be Sharp (1981) and Hart (1987)).

Recognition must be granted that any economic analysis of time at work is at best partial, and is predicated on the assumption that the individual/organization has a degree of choice in the adoption of working-time arrangements. That such discretion may be unrealistic is easily demonstrated. Brown *et al* (1984) for example found that 80 per cent of sample workers were unable to work overtime hours even if they so desired. Moreover as Blyton and Hassard show in this volume, the economic allocation of working-time is a problem particular to one stage in the historical development of the economy. Indeed, writers of the 1970s saw the advent of technological change as initiating a new period of leisure, so that a surplus (rather than shortage) of time became the focus of attention (Jenkins and Sherman 1979). The economic recession of the 1980s seems to have put paid to such speculation, with any increase in non-worktime being concentrated on the unemployed rather than evenly distributed.

The economic allocation of time remains a conceptual and practical problem. It is to the clarification of this problem that this chapter is addressed.

THE INCOME/LEISURE TRADE OFF

The economic analysis of time at work has developed as a subset of the economic theory of factor pricing, which is iself a component part of the economic theory of price (Koutsoyiannis 1975: 35–8; Chacholiades 1986: 126–33; Ballante and Jackson 1979; 48–62). Within this neoclassical approach, individuals choose the income/working time combination from the set of available opportunities that best matches their preferences between the satisfaction derived from goods bought through income and that generated by the availability of non-work (leisure) time. Competition in the product and factor markets then ensures that employers offer income/working-time alternatives that accord with these preferences through the familiar competitive process of reducing factor costs (and thereby increasing profits) for employers quick enough to respond to the changing preferences of present (and potential) employees (Hicks 1932).

At its simplest, the theory can be explained via the use of indifference curves. Assume that the wage rate per hour is fixed at w, and that the individual can choose the precise number of hours to work. Then the income/leisure constraint or budget line is a straight line between income of 24w (and no leisure time) and 24 hours of leisure (but no income), Figure 4.1. Since both income and leisure time give positive utility, a trade-off must be made, depending on the individual's strength of preference btween them.[1] This preference can be expressed in terms of an indifference curve, showing combinations of income and leisure that give rise to the same total level of satisfaction (utility). Utility is maximized when the indifference curve is at a tangent to the income/leisure constraint (point C in Figure 1). The individual then works 24-D hours, receives an income equal to OE and enjoys OD hours of leisure (non-work time) per day.

Figure 1 The income leisure trade-off

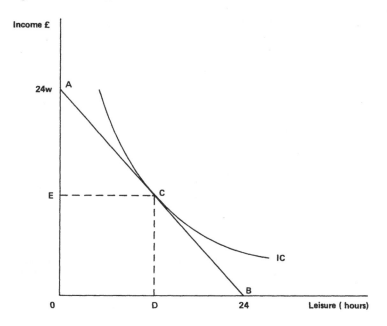

59

Figure 2 Overtime premium

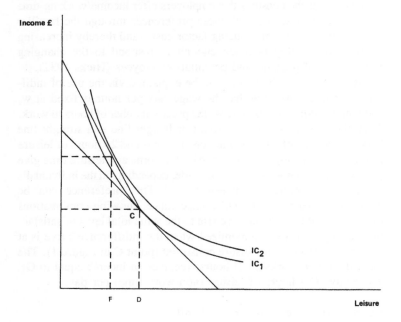

Figure 3 Non-wage income

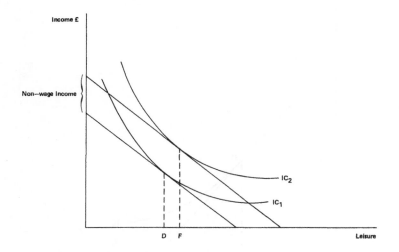

This income/leisure model can be used to develop several unambiguous predictions:

(1) An overtime premium paid for hours worked beyond 24-D will lead to longer working. In Figure 2, the income/leisure constraint becomes steeper at C, allowing the individual to increase total utility (reaching IC_2) by working 24-F hours.

(2) The convexity of indifference curves ensures that the existence of non-wage income will reduce hours of work.[2] Non-wage income shifts the income/leisure constraint upwards, leading to a fall in worked hours (from 24-D to 24-F in Figure 3).

Thus a change in the wage rate has both a relative price and an income effect. Ambiguity arises because these effects may influence hours worked in opposite directions.

The situation is illustrated in Figure 4. An increase in the wage rate pivots the income/leisure constraint on the income axis. The individual worker starts at point C, working 24-D hours and ends up at point E, working 24-F hours. The income and relative price (substitution) effects of the wage rate change can be separated by first making a compensating variation in real income by shifting the new income/leisure constraint line downwards until it is tangential to the

Figure 4 Effects of a wage rate change

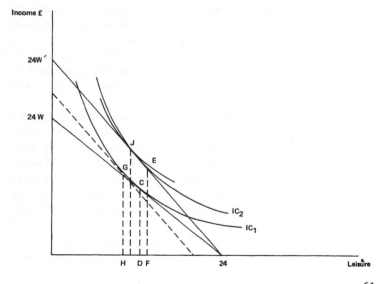

original indifference curve. Points C and G are on the same indifference curve and therefore show equal levels of total satisfaction (real income). The difference between C and G is solely due to the increase in the relative price of leisure (slope of the income/leisure constraint). The difference between points G and E is then due solely to the difference in income (since the income/leisure constraints have the same slope). The movement from C to G is then the substitution effect, showing that the increased relative price of leisure will lead to a substitution of work (income) for leisure. The movement from G to E is the income effect, and shows a fall in the demand for worktime (increase in leisure) as a result of higher income.

The net result is the sum of the income and substitution effects. As drawn in Figure 4, the income effect outweighs the substitution effect, so that hours worked fall. However, it is possible that the final equilibrium point could have been at J, where the income effect is insufficient to outweigh the substitution effect and rise in hours of work. It is the possible contra-indications of the income and substitution effects that make unambiguous predictions impossible (Robbins 1930). Since rising real wage rates have been a consistent reality of economic development (Denison 1962), this ambiguity has led to the income/leisure choice model being reformulated in a number of ways.

PRODUCTIVITY AND HOURS OF WORK

Barzel (1973) traces the development of the formalized model back to Hicks (1932), to point out that the income/leisure model outlined above implicitly assumes that daily hours of work have no effect on productivity per hour, and are thereby treated as homogeneous by the employer, who is then indifferent between various numbers of worker/average working hours combinations that yield the same aggregate labour hours worked.

Given competitive product and factor market conditions, the equilibrium wage rate will be where the wage is equal to the value of the marginal product.[3] Then to analyse hours per day it is necessary to examine how productivity varies with the length of working hours. Barzel assumes that marginal product rises during early hours of the working day, reaches a maximum and then falls with subsequent hours. The value of the daily product curve[4] (VDP) will then be as drawn in Figure 5.

The effect of allowing productivity to vary with hours is to eliminate the linearity of the income/leisure constraint. The equilibrium

Figure 5 Equilibrium hours when productivity varies

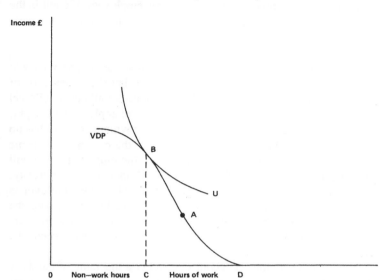

position is again determined by the point of tangency between the individual's indifference curve (U, reflecting preferences) and the opportunity set represented by the income/leisure constraint (now labelled VDP). In Figure 5 the individual works CD hours, and makes a contribution to the net value of the firm of BC.

Given competitive product and factor market conditions, wages per day (of different lengths) will depend on the supply and demand of workers choosing particular income/leisure combinations. Suppose that in Figure 5, a group of workers currently employed at point A develops a preference for income rather than leisure, so that they would rather move to point B. Since they would be better off at B, there will be an excess supply of workers at B and shortages at A. Wages (per day) at B must fall, and firms operating at B will earn excess profits, inducing other firms to offer B rather than A.

The Barzel model has several implications:

(1) Even if all workers have the same productivities (VDP curves), variations in tastes will ensure that hours/income combinations offered by firms will be non-uniform.

(2) The observed hourly wage will differ amongst those working different hours. For example, employee preference for part-time work will ensure that hourly part-time wage rates lie below the

hourly rate of full-time equivalent employees. Then the higher average hourly productivity of part-time employees implicit in the VDP curve is outweighed by the employee preferences for part-time work.

The employment contract of the typical employee pre-specifies both daily wage rates and daily hours. 'Average hourly wages can, of course, be calculated but have little operational significance' (Barzel 1973: 224). This average hourly wage does not apply at the margin, since overtime rates are higher, and the employment contract has no provision for working less time. In practice the option of overtime working at a predetermined rate rests with the employer, who will only offer overtime when the value of work increases temporarily. The agreed overtime rate reflects the rate at which the employee is prepared to transform leisure hours into extra income, given the normal length of working day. The employer then exercises his overtime discretion whenever the value of overtime working exceeds the extra cost.

Note that by combining labour demand (via the value of the daily product) and labour supply (via individual preferences), wages per day are determined endogenously. Then wages can change only as a result of changes in productivity or product prices (shifting VDP) or through changes in income/leisure preferences. Non-wage costs of labour will shift VDP downwards, whilst increases in labour productivity or product prices will lead the VDP curve to pivot upwards on the income axis. As in the simple income/leisure model, the existence of non-wage income will move the income/leisure constraint upwards by the amount of that income, leading to a fall in hours worked (if the income elasticity of demand for leisure is positive).

As noted, the relationship between average hourly wage rate and daily hours worked depends on the position on VDP that the individual chooses to work. Below point B in Figure 5, the productivity of the last hour of work exceeds average productivity per hour so that the fewer hours the individual chooses to work, the lower the average hourly wage. To the left of point B, the converse applies (since at B the marginal product per hour is equal to average product per hour).[5]

Feldstein (1967) estimated that for a cross-section of British industries the elasticity of output with respect to hours is some 1.5–2.0 times larger than that of output with respect to the number of workers. This implies that the ratio of marginal to average product per hour exceeds that per person, which in turn suggests that employers are more likely to seek overtime than extra workers to meet an upsurge in product demand.

The conclusion from the Barzel model is that differential average hourly wage rates may do no more than reflect the uneven preferences of employees towards different working-time arrangements. Attempts to increase the hourly wage of part-time employees in line with their full time equivalents may simply lead to the oversupply of part-time workers.

THE EMPLOYMENT/HOURS CHOICE

Brechling (1965) examined the income/leisure choice from the employer's perspective by pointing out that demand for labour time is a demand for effective labour services, where labour services has a number of dimensions, such as numbers employed, average hours of work, intensity of effort, etc. The level of effective labour services (S) is the product of the numbers employed (E) and some index of labour utilization (U). Then the numbers employed, average hours of work and intensity of effort are substitute inputs in the production of labour services. The actual choice between employment, hours, and effort depends on the relative prices of each dimension of labour services. Thus the employer will seek whatever combination can provide the desired level of labour services at lowest cost. Consider, for example, the distribution between hours worked and employment (Hill 1989). A given level of labour services could be achieved with a particular number of employees working a certain number of hours, or with fewer people each working longer average hours. The analysis can be conducted in terms of isoquants, showing the possible combinations of inputs to produce a particular output level (desired level of labour services). Since numbers employed and average hours worked are imperfect substitutes (because of productivity variations per person and per hour), the isoquant will be convex to the origin (Figure 6).

The choice of average hours/numbers employed will then depend on the relative prices of each. Brechling analyses a payment system of a standard hourly wage rate up to 'normal' hours of work, with a premium rate for hours worked beyond this. Then the isocost line, showing combinations purchasable with a fixed monetary sum, will be kinked at the level of normal hours (line ABC in Figure 6). Given this payment system, and desired labour services Q_1, N_1 people will be employed for H_1 hours each. As drawn, tangency occurs when

65

Figure 6 Distribution of workers/average hours

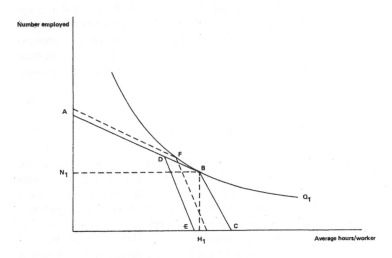

actual hours equal normal hours (and no overtime is worked). Suppose instead that normal hours were reduced, so that the overtime premium is paid earlier. The isocost line then becomes ADE, and labour services Q_1 are no longer achievable with this money outlay. If labour services Q_1 are still desired, expenditure must increase (moving ADE outwards parallel to itself) until Q_1 is reached (at point F). At F employment has increased and average hours have fallen compared to point B. Note that some overtime is now worked.

The conclusions from the Brechling model are that both employment and average hours depend on the degree of substitution between these labour dimensions and the relative cost of each. The relative cost of each depends in turn upon the payment system adopted and the extent of any overtime premium. For example, the existence of non-wage costs of labour would shift point A in Figure 6 downwards and be liable to increase average hours worked. What the Brechling model achieves is to point to the factors that determine the consequences of a change in hours (i.e. the substitutability and relative price of labour dimensions).

CAPITAL UTILIZATION

Given the simplifying assumption of just two inputs (capital and labour), the mirror image of the income/leisure choice is the capital utilization decision. In the mid 1960s, the economic theory of capital utilization received a severe jolt with the publication of papers by Foss (1963) and Marris (1964). In the former Foss reported that capital utilization had increased but that the highest level of utilization reached was just 23 per cent — equivalent to a 38-hour week. Hence American manufacturing capacity was idle more than three-quarters of available time. In the latter paper Marris found that firms planned to leave capital idle most of the time as a rational part of their investment decisions.

Hence idle capacity was a rational economic decision, depending on the costs of using plant and the demand for products. The usual justification for unused capacity was unforeseen changes in tastes and preferences, leading to demand deficiency. Thus capital idleness was the consequence of unfulfilled expectations.

More important than these reasons, was that of rhythmic input prices. Winston (1974) summarizes the argument in terms of input differences:

(1) Factor ownership institutions vary, so that some factors are bought as stocks (capital equipment) whilst others are purchased as flows (labour time).
(2) The utilization of a factor stock can be changed at the discretion of the factor owner.
(3) Periods of co-operation between factors are often mismatched.
(4) The prices of some factor services vary rhythmically.

Thus the decision about factor utilization is made by the owner of the factor. The owner of capital stocks or the owner's representative (manager) decides on capital use, whilst the owners of labour services (workers) choose a particular utilization rate for their labour (via the income/leisure choice model). Capital utilization then requires the congruence of these decisions. Then capital is left idle for much of the time because the income/leisure choice determines that labour will be more expensive at unsocial hours (such as evenings and weekends). In choosing a level of plant, the manager has rationally decided that because of these variations in the cost of labour per hour, profit maximization (or cost minimization) dictates that planned output will be produced at times of (relative) cheapness of other inputs.

The rhythmic input price argument is easily extended to inputs other than labour. Electricity may be cheaper at certain periods, light and warmth may be available cheaply (or even for free) during the day but be expensive to create at night, etc (Stigler and Kindahl 1970). Thus:

> Higher utilization will always lower average capital costs per unit since capital will be owned by the firm whether used or not; but higher utilization will also raise the average costs of the rhythmic input, for instance, average labour costs, so that the level of utilization that optimally will be built into the capital stock *ex ante* will just balance capital savings with rhythmic cost increases: an increase in utilization beyond the optimum would increase the rhythmic input cost more than it would reduce capital costs.
>
> (Winston 1974: 1306)

The actual utilization rate chosen will depend on relative factor prices, the amplitude of the input price rhythm, the capital intensity of production and the elasticity of factor substitution. Thus, if capital is expensive relative to labour, high capital utilization will be required to reduce the average cost of capital per unit of output. If the over-time premium is high, firms have an incentive to operate only at low-cost periods, thereby planning low levels of capital utilization. The capital intensity argument is similar to the high relative cost of capital argument, since a high capital intensity of production provides an incentive to economize on the cost of capital by using equipment as much as possible. Finally, the possibility of factor substitution reduces the influence of relative factor prices in determining the capital utilization level.

HOURS OF WORK

The time-at-work decision has now been examined from a number of perspectives: by looking at the individual income/leisure choice, by allowing productivity per hour to vary, by examining the various dimensions of labour services and by considering labour utilization as the mirror image of capital utilization. A number of useful insights have been reached, but no general model as yet exists of working time that integrates variations in productivity, preferences, or payment systems. Such a general model would indeed permit testable hypothesis about the relationship between productivity, wages, preferences, and working time, but a model of this nature remains some way off (although some tentative steps were taken by Hill (1984)).

The inability of economic theory to generate such a model is most obvious in the failure to develop unambiguous predictions about the consequences for working time of increases in the real wage rate. Empirically the relationship between average hours and real wage rates is less than clear. Sharp (1981) reports that average weekly hours for both full-time men and women in British manufacturing fell by about 10 per cent between 1956 and 1978, whilst real average weekly wages rose by 155 per cent and 180 per cent for men and women respectively over the same period.[6] Owen (1979) argues that for the United States, average weekly hours fell some 50 per cent between 1900 and 1950, but with little change since then (the so-called levelling-off problem). It is relatively easy to argue that rising real wages resulted in both rising incomes and greater leisure time, but since 1950 in the US it appears that most of the benefits from rising real wage rates have been taken in the form of extra income.

A fall in average weekly hours is easily explained by the income/leisure trade-off model. As the wage rate rose, the income effect was to induce workers to demand more leisure time, and competitive factor and product market conditions ensured that this demand was met by employers. However, the substitution effect was important in ensuring that only a part of increased income opportunities was transformed with leisure time, since higher wage rates raised the opportunity cost of leisure. Owen (1979) reports estimates that in the late nineteenth and early twentieth centuries, less than one-quarter of the potential growth in consumption went to reduced hours of work. However, the income/leisure choice model failed to predict the levelling-off of working hours in the US, and says little about the current relative stability of working time.

At least a part of the failure to offer a full explanation of working-time changes can be traced to the convention of regarding working time as being of a somewhat different nature to non-work time, connected only in the sense that time not at work is simply available time minus time at work. More recently, however, economists have begun to develop a more general approach to time that recognises the interdependence and symmetries between worktime and non-work time (DeSerpa 1971; Sharp 1981).

ALLOCATION OF TIME

The neoclassical approach sees the standard worker trading off the desire for more goods (through more work and hence more income) against the desire for leisure time. In 1965 Gary Becker widened the argument by pointing out that consumption, like the generation of income, also took time. Satisfaction was generated by the combination of market goods plus non-work time. Moreover some non-work activities were essentially productive, involving the combination of various inputs to produce (enjoyable or essential) output, just as some worktime was essentially consumption activity. Not only did goods differ in their relative money prices but also in the relative time involved in consumption. Time and market goods may be substitutes or complements. For example, processed foods are more expensive but less time-intensive than their natural counterparts. High-income consumers, with a greater opportunity cost of nonwork time, would purchase less time-intensive goods than either low-income earners or the unemployed. They would also have an incentive to substitute the time of others for their own (relatively expensive) time, for example by eating out, hiring maids or childcare assistants. Becker showed that as the wage rate increased, the ratio of market goods input to consumption time input must rise, leading the consumer to substitute goods for time (Becker 1965).

Becker's analysis has a number of profound implications for hours of work, education, the productivity of service industries, and the household division of labour, amongst others (see for example Blaug 1976; Sharp 1981; Ghez and Becker 1975). For the purposes of this book, it is the implications for working-time that are most relevant. The starting point for analysis is that different goods require different time periods for their 'household' production and consumption and therefore have varying opportunity costs in terms of forgone earnings. Then, for example, a rise in non-wage income would increase the consumption of most commodities, thereby increasing the time required for consumption and reducing hours of work (as in the simple income/leisure model). However, hours of work could stay constant or increase if the extra income led to the substitution of less time-intensive commodities for relatively time-intensive ones (and relatively time-intensive goods were inferior in the sense of having negative income elasticities) (Becker 1965: 501).

It is fundamental to demand theory that a rise in income leaves relative prices unchanged, and thus has no substitution effects on the demand for various goods. However, since goods require time for their consumption, a rise in income would change the relative price of goods in terms of forgone earnings. Hence an increase in income increases the relative total price (money plus time) of relatively time-intensive goods, and therefore leads to their substitution by less time-intensive goods.

If we distinguish between goods and commodities by allowing commodities to refer to utility-generating activities (goods plus time), a rise in earnings leads to the substitution of time-intensive commodities by goods-intensive ones. A shift away from time-intensive goods could result in a fall in the time spent in consumption and therefore an increase in the time spent at work. Moreover the cost of commodities is not simply the sum of time plus money, because the value of time itself (in terms of forgone earnings) varies according to when it occurs. The value of time may be lower at weekends and evenings because of the absence of opportunities to transform time into earnings.[7]

HOUSEHOLD DISTRIBUTION OF TIME

Theories of the allocation of time have led economists to consider the distribution of time and activities within the household. Empirical evidence on 'time budgets' shows some surprising results. Vanek (1973) showed that the time spent by full-time housewives at housework changed very little in the period 1920–70. The rapid growth of female part-time employment (Hill 1987) together with evidence of the increasing household production activities of many men (Robinson and Converse 1967), may imply that for many people the quantity of pure leisure time may have decreased. Sharp (1981) analysed the results of a multinational survey of time-use in twelve countries, to produce the following table.

Table 1 Average time allocated to activities per day

		minutes	%
1	Work plus travel to work	302.1	21
2	Housework	159.7	11.1
3	Other household obligations	42.4	2.9
4	Childcare	29.3	2.0
5	Sleeping, eating, and personal care	621.5	43.2
6	Non-work travel	37.4	2.6
7	Study and group activity	25.3	1.7
8	Media (TV, newspapers, etc.)	105.5	7.3
9	Social and leisure	116.9	8.1

Source: Sharpe (1981) derived from Szalai (1972)

Note that Table 1 lists overall averages over a seven-day period involving fifteen communities in twelve countries, ranging from Peru to Hungary via the US. Sharp points out that such 'aggregate' averages

71

have severe difficulties of interpretation, but the figures do point to a general lack of leisure time overall, casting considerable doubt on the choice of leisure as the alternative to income-generating employment. The evidence is in sharp contrast to the conventional wisdom of the 1960s and 70s, which saw the introduction and widespread adoption of labour-saving household devices as heralding a new freedom from household drudgery (an idea first proposed by Long 1958).

The time-allocation model has been extended in a number of ways to explain the distribution of time between work, leisure and household production (see for example Gronau 1977, or Michael and Becker 1973). Figure 7 provides a simple diagramatic representation of the time-allocation decision (derived from Owen, 1979).

Figure 7 Total time allocation

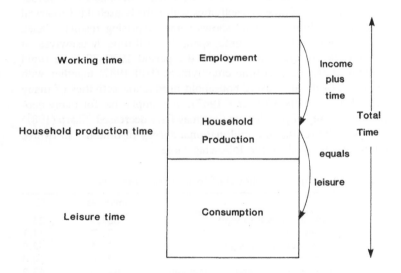

Total time (K) is divided between three activities: employment time (M), household production time (H), and leisure time (L). With an hourly wage of w, total income Y is wM, used to buy goods and services P which are then combined with household production time to generate commodities A, enjoyed during leisure time L. Then in each sector, labour-time is combined with goods or services to generate output. The problem to be solved is what happens to the distribution of time between consumption and household production if hours of work remain roughly constant whilst the real wage rate rises.

The principles of marginalism dictate that time will be divided between activities so that an extra hour spent on one yields the same satisfaction as an extra hour spent on any other. The consequence of increased income then depends on the change in the marginal contribution of extra time spent on household production compared to that from extra time spent on consumption. If the provision of extra goods and services raises the productivity of household production time compared to consumption time, production time will increase and consumption time must decrease. However, the rise in the output of commodities (generated by increased goods and services plus household production time) will increase the demand for leisure time in which to enjoy those commodities. The net effects depend on the relative substitution possibilities. As income increases (and keeping working hours constant), either more income has to be used per hour of household production time, or more household production time must be used per hour of leisure time (or some combination of the two). The net effect upon leisure time depends on the possibility of increasing the ratio of goods to time in household production relative to the opportunities for increasing the ratio of commodities to leisure time in consumption. Owen concludes that the stability of leisure time suggests that the two substitution possibilities are roughly similar in magnitude (Owen 1979: 36).

The time-allocation model enables further conclusions to be drawn about temporal allocations in contemporary life. For example, the introduction of household time-saving devices (timesavers) has generally led to an increase in household production activity rather than to any increases in leisure time. For example, the widespread ownership of motor cars, instead of reducing time spent travelling to work, has enabled workers to reside further from the work place (and hence benefit from reductions in the relative cost of housing, as well as quality improvements).

The time-allocation model represented in Figure 7 extends the alternatives available far beyond those implied by the simple income/leisure trade-off. The income/leisure model allows increases in wage rates to lead either to reductions in working time (increases in leisure) or to increases in consumption. The time-allocation model extends this choice to include improved conditions of employment or household production, reduced time at household production or increased leisure time, or even any combination between alternatives. The actual choice made will depend on the relative satisfaction from each activity, the productivity of time or material inputs in each, and the relative cost of inputs. For example, continual improvements in household production conditions have reduced the satisfaction of further improvements relative to that obtained from improved working conditions, so that some of an increase in wage rates is taken in improved work environments.

The time-allocation model, however, whilst being a welcome extension of the income/leisure choice, raises a similar number of ambiguities and questions. Once more the net effects of a rise in real wages are uncertain — the best we can do is to point to the likely determining factors. Moreover, whilst the employment/household production/leisure time distinction is an improvement on the simple work/leisure choice, ambiguity remains in the definition of various activities. For example the simple activity of reading a book could be work, household production or leisure (perhaps a technical manual, recipe book or novel respectively). Work itself may be perceived by some as an intrinsically rewarding experience (see Starkey in this volume) giving meaning, substance and order to everyday life. The point is that the categorization of time could continue indefinitely, but are the gains in understanding outweighing the loss through increased complexity?

Note also that the analysis has proceeded outside the institutional/legal/social framework that constrains the time-allocation decision. Extending the individual time-allocation decision to the household raises questions about the division of labour and comparative advantage that the economist is ill-equipped to answer.

THE RELATIVE RETURN TO EFFORT

We have already noted the inability of the simple income/leisure choice model to explain the (relative) stability of American average working hours in recent decades. Owen (1979) has made an interesting attempt to explain this levelling-off in terms of the concept of the relative return to effort, or the ratio of the marginal-to-average return to effort. It is Owen's contention that it is the elasticity of income with respect to effort, rather than the absolute level of income, which is the determining factor in the supply of effort. Thus for example, in physically demanding jobs, this will mean that the marginal return on an extra hour's work will be low (given that long hours are worked already), so that as hours increase, the relative return for effort diminishes (note the similarity to the Barzel model outlined above).

The argument is that the relative return for effort will dictate changes in the hours of work. In the nineteenth and early twentieth centuries, the productive consumption effect ensured that the relative return for effort remained high,[8] but by the mid-twentieth century the productive consumption effect had both diminished and been offset by the emergence of a training and education effect.

In a subsistence economy, the relative return to effort is very high, since the worker must put in long hours to survive. As wages increase, the need for long hours diminishes, but income still has a productive consumption effect in that extra consumption increases the capacity for work, so that an extra hour's work increases both current and future income. As wage rates continue to increase, the productive consumption effect lessens, and the pressure for working-time reductions increases, rewarding those firms offering lower working times. However, further increases in wage rates ultimately reduce the productive consumption effect to approximately zero, so that pressure for further working-time reductions disappears.

Finally, investment in education and training increase the relative return to effort, compensating for consumption forgone during the training period by raising the hourly wage rate for the educated worker. The worker then has a clear incentive to spread the cost of training over longer hours of work. Owen estimated the elasticity of hours worked with respect to the hourly wage and real educational costs to be -0.2 and $+0.1$ respectively, implying that increases in wages reduce hours of work whilst increases in educational costs increase them. In the post-war period, education costs increased at a faster rate than wages, due both to the baby boom and the rapid lengthening of average educational duration (Lindsay 1971), so that changes in hourly wages and education costs have offset each other to leave hours of work relatively stable.

CONCLUSIONS AND POLICY ISSUES

The primary conclusion from any economic analysis of time and work decisions must be the negative one that economic theory has failed in the task of yielding unambiguous conclusions about the effect on working-time of changes in parameters such as real wage rates, and the productivity of labour and capital. However, such a conclusion exaggerates the purpose of economic theory, and undervalues the insights generated by the pursuit of explanation. The economic analysis of time at work has yielded a number of important propositions that are of substantial theoretical and empirical relevance in the description and understanding of labour market processes.

The simplest income/leisure choice model concluded that at the optimum, the marginal rate of transformation between income and leisure time equalled the individual's marginal rate of substitution between them. Such a model, while not suffering from 'excessive generality', did emphasize the income and substitution effects of wage changes. The introduction of productivity and preference effects firmly established an economic rationale for differential hourly wage rates for worker groups with varying preferences towards working-time arrangements, that owed nothing to concepts of discrimination or injustice. Extending the model to define labour services as the product of both numbers employed and intensity (or duration) of effort showed the importance of payment systems and normal hours in determining both employment and average work duration and hence introduced an institutional dimension into the analysis, capable of explaining the employment consequences of various employment contracts in terms of the degree of substitution between labour dimensions and the relative cost of each.

The capital utilization decision was developed as the mirror image of labour utilization, and the under-utilization of capital explained in terms of rhythmic input prices and factor ownership institutions. Finally the working-time decision was shown to be a subset of a total time allocation system, which took account of the necessary interdependencies between arbitrarily defined categorizations of time such as work, leisure and household production. A full exploration of time-allocation requires these interdependencies to be made explicit, and showed that the impact of rising real hourly wage rates depended on the substitutability of time, money, and commodities in all three time categories. Each activity (work, leisure, and household production) involved elements of both production and consumption, differing only in ratio. Thus for example, the earlier definition of leisure (time not at work) was a simplification that may hinder explanation. The total time-allocation model was seen to be extendable to areas such as education and training.

The latter part of the 1980s has seen the development of a number of labour market phenomena which can be explained in terms of the foregoing analysis. For example the rapid growth of (predominantly female) part-time work in contemporary Britain can be seen as the result of the escalating cost and productivity of capital equipment (and the commensurate desire to extend utilization), the growth of time-specific production activities (i.e. the rise of service industries) and the preparedness of some worker groups to see working-time preferences reflected in lower hourly wage rates. Note, however, that the absence of full-time employment alternatives is clearly a factor in explaining such preparedness.

Similar comments apply to the growth of labour-market flexibility, whether judged by function or numerically. The management desire for flexibility is founded on the increased uncertainty surrounding input prices, production possibilities, and product demand, largely as a result of the coincidence of economic depression and the development of new technology (Hill and Blyton 1987). Such changes, often stylized as the demise of mass production technologies in favour of production processes which are rapidly switchable and extendable, seek to shift the burden of uncertainty from the owners of capital to the owners of labour-power and are only sustainable in the absence of alternative (more secure) employment opportunities.

The analysis thus far presented has had little to say about labour-market realities such as overtime working, the effects of shiftwork, retirement options, etc. However it is our contention that each of these labour-market dimensions can be successfully analysed in terms of the models presented. It is left to the interested reader to pursue such interests. What the analysis has done is to draw attention to the fundamental economic variables that are liable to be important in any such analysis.

The final point to note is to re-emphasize the fact that the realities of time at work decisions are severely constrained by the institutional and legal framework that defines our society. An understanding of that framework is left to the companion essays in sociology and industrial relations, whilst the factors underlying employee (and employer) preferences towards alternative working arrangements are explored in the chapter on the psychology of work.

NOTES

1. Slightly more sophisticated approaches see some non-work time as 'productive consumption', essential for work performance (DeSerpa 1971). The notion of productive consumption will be developed further.

2. Since work is an inferior good (i.e. it has negative income elasticity).

3. Let total revenue be the product of price times quantity (PQ) whilst total cost is the sum of labour and capital costs (wL + rK), with capital fixed at K.

Then profit $\pi = PQ - wL - rK$

and $\delta\pi/\delta Q = P - w \, \delta L/\delta Q = 0$, so $P = w\delta L/\delta Q$ and $w = P\delta Q/\delta L$ i.e. the wage rate is equal to price times the marginal product of labour.

4. This is just the marginal product of labour/hour curve, laterally

inverted and multiplied by the constant product price.

5. The output elasticity with respect to input x is defined as

$$\varepsilon_x = \delta Q/\delta X . X/Q$$

and is equal to the ratio of marginal to average products for that input. Then at B, $\varepsilon_L = 1$; whilst to the right of B, $\varepsilon_L > 1$.

6. This implies an hours elasticity with respect to real wages of about -0.06.

7. Although Becker points out that if the opportunity for weekend or evening work exists, the cost of time may be higher then (Becker 1965: 503). Evidence for Britain suggests an average shift premium in the region of 20 per cent (National Board for Prices and Incomes, 1970).

8. Recall that productive consumption refers to the impact on labour productivity of attaining a certain minimum standard of consumption.

5

Time and organization

John Hassard

INTRODUCTION

In this chapter, we consider temporal aspects of organization. However, we use this term in its broadest sense. We assess matters of physiological and social organizing as well as the organization of manufacturing and service systems: we discuss natural and cultural times as well as those relevant to industrial and commercial enterprise.

The chapter commences with an examination of human-time (part one). That is, with a discussion of time as intrinsic to both the human and the social being. We argue that the natural times which humans experience from birth become modified within a system of culturally sanctioned social times. We describe how individuals become socialized by complex patterns of temporal structuring, and how they learn time-discipline through membership of formal organizations such as the family and the school — agencies which prepare them for the organization demanding the greatest time-discipline of all, the work-place. Finally, we note how on gaining entry into a work-place, individuals embark upon a 'career' — a process which sees them constantly evaluated in time-related terms.

In part two, the focus shifts to 'organizations in themselves'. The ontological emphasis changes as organizations are portrayed as systems which have time problems of their own. We look specifically at the temporal resources of work organizations, and assess the difficulties such institutions face in controlling temporal assets. We draw upon the works of Moore (1963a), Lauer (1980), and McGrath and Rotchford (1983), in describing the measures organizations take for resolving problems of scheduling, allocation and synchronization.

We begin the chapter, however, with some basics. First we outline two themes which underpin the chapter. These summarize the main theoretical positions adopted in the analysis. Following this, we start the chapter proper by introducing some of the natural and social imperatives underlying the relationship between time and organization. These imperatives build upon the two analytical themes to form a basis for the descriptions of time and organization which follow.

Chapter Themes

Time is a basic element of human organization. We argue that although temporality may lack meaning unless we accept it as a stream of motion and action, for much human understanding it also represents a structured condition of behaviour — a boundary for defining and stabilizing existence. Temporal units are both physically determined and socially constructed. Although the physical properties of the daily cycle presuppose several natural differentiations (e.g. day-time and night-time, work-time and rest-time, sleeping-time and waking-time), other intervals are more arbitarily and artificially defined (e.g. seconds, minutes, and hours). In sum, Theme 1 suggests that although man has time forced upon him, he is nevertheless still master of its description.

It is the very fact of man's biological and thus ultimately finite existence that compels him to 'organize' time. As time cannot be conserved nor cultivated, it must be organized. The finite nature of human-time means that it must be sub-divided and prioritized. Because of this, social as well as biological agencies must be created in order to harness temporal potential and make it productive. Humans have to develop abstract as well as organic modes of organization in order to adapt to the temporal constraints of their social and natural environments. In sum, Theme 2 suggests that human activities are governed by times which are both natural and social — times which are central to physical and cultural wellbeing; times which are fundamental to the development of concrete and abstract forms of organizing.

PART ONE: TIME AND HUMAN ORGANIZATION

While in this chapter we devote most of our analysis to social times, we must remember that it is in fact nature which first gives humans their sense of time: it is the natural cycles of human development

80

which first signal that there are patterns to life.

Natural Times: Physiology and Temporal Entrainment

The most pervasive and primary of natural cycles are those associated with human physiology. Biological science has long discussed the rhythmicality of bodily functions and described the cyclical nature of much physiological behaviour. Biologists have argued that such rhythmical patterning is an expression of the so-called 'internal' clocks which are a basic feature of all living systems.

Indeed, natural cycles are found to govern whole ranges of organic functions and responses; as for example conception, pulse, digestion, respiration, growth, menstruation, and age. Temporal recursiveness forms a dominant metaphor at all levels of biological analysis, from micro to macro. While for the former it provides an infrastructure for our physiological clocks, that is, through notion of cellular and metabolic rates; for the latter it dominates our conception of, for example, the species life-cycle, the personal life-cycle, and diurnal and sub-diurnal rhythms.

Of such cycles, however, it is a particular form of diurnal rhythm — the 'circadian rhythm' — which is of the most interest to us, for it is this cycle which, in recent years, has been associated with problems of employee health and welfare. It is the concept of circadian rhythm which — together with the related notion of 'entrainment' — has helped to explain important links between physiological cycles and work-related illnesses; as for example the costs to health in deploying particular forms of shift and task systems (Browne 1949; Colquhoun, Blake, and Edwards 1968; Colquhoun 1970).

Circadian Rhythms. Research on circadian rhythms has shown how, under carefully controlled scientific conditions, the operation of the physiological clock proves to be independent of human clock-time. Experiments have shown how many features of physiological and behavioural functioning operate within their own cycles of 'circa' 24 hours.[1] While under normal conditions many of these features appear to be determined by the day/night cycle of the earth's rotation, experiments have shown how they are essentially free-running.

However, while such rhythms can be said to be free-running, they are, nevertheless, if not determined, at least regulated by cycles of daily activity. Indeed, central to the notion of circadian rhythm is that of diurnal entrainment — the idea that certain endogenous cycles are

81

appropriated by, and come to operate in rhythm with, exogenous ones (Pittendrigh 1972). By this, we mean a process whereby an endogenous cycle (e.g. a physiological function) comes to have the same, or at least a very similar, rhythm to that of an exogenous cycle (e.g. the day/night cycle). Although we can never say that the exogenous cycle has caused the new cycle — for the cycle is endogenous — we can say at least that it has modified it.

It is, in fact, because of this phenomenon that many endogenous, physiological cycles come to be regulated by the exogenous cycle of day and night.

Due to these great conditioning effects of temporal entrainment, scientists now suggest that when we disrupt normal diurnal cycles, we may in fact be inducing many potentially adverse physiological responses. Concern has been raised, for example, over the possible harmful affects to physiological functioning brought about by requiring employees to exchange their usual day-work/night-rest patterns to ones which are the reverse. Linked to this have been worries over the extent to which such disruptions affect both employee attitudes (e.g. job satisfaction and life satisfaction) and work behaviours (e.g. increases in accident and sickness rates). Scientists have become increasingly concerned about the long-term effects of temporal oscillations; and especially those related to frequent changes in time-zone or in repeated inversions of activity-sleep cycles.

In the wake of this, then, a major project for organizational research is to gather detailed information on the physiological, attitudinal, and behavioural costs of disruptions to diurnal rhythms. In particular, we need data on how individuals differ both in terms of their degrees of entrainment to the day/night cycle, and in their tolerance of disruptions to it.

Social Times: Coming to Terms with Organization

Let us now turn to the second of our imperatives — social times. We have said that a sense of time is an inherent quality of human life. And that the sheer nature of existence prompts awareness of temporal differences between, for example, hunger and satisfaction, comfort and pain, and waking and dreaming. We have suggested, also, that we first place structure on existence by assimilating times which have a natural and physiological basis.

However, despite the potency of such natural times, we must remember also that many of our physiological times become linked, inextricably, to social times. For example, as a growing infant can survive only briefly without liquid, food, and clothing, it is forced to place a constant set of temporal requirements on those around it — on its wider society. As the infant is unable to sustain life unaided, its physical wellbeing becomes dependent not only on its own capacity to demand, but also on the willingness of those responsible for it to meet such demands. Given the nature of this relationship, the infant has no other choice than to allow the timing of its demands to be regulated by social convention. Gradually its needs become influenced by social constraints — i.e. constraints which dictate 'correct' times for food, drink, sleep, etc. As the process of physical development is joined by social development, so the infant begins to appreciate time as a vehicle which brings it within the orbit of human organization.

Social Organization. Therefore, so that individuals may function adequately in society, they must come to terms with the temporality which underlies social organization. Although physiological time-needs persist throughout life, and while there are limits to the social ingenuity which can be placed upon their structuring, nevertheless social convention comes in time to regulate their satisfaction. The dominance of the physiological as the basis for action is seen to moderate and then to decline as the individual matures. Physiological demand gives way to social performance: biological decree succumbs to social negotiation. While our sense of temporality is founded on the biology of the human organism, it becomes refined and ordered by participation in society and culture. In maturation, individuals learn to organize temporal experience in accordance with particular social and cultural processes.

The Family. For the infant, the temporal parameters of its actions become modified from their basis in physiological need to a new locus in the normative structures of an organization — the family. The development of social relations with parents and siblings signals that experience has become increasingly controlled, and that the infant has grasped a sense of organization. The acceptance of normative constraints sees its physiological needs — e.g. for multiple feeds, or for sleeping during the middle of the day — deferred in favour of alternative possibilities (e.g. play). Through time, the infant becomes aware of how its actions are organized into formal patterns by agents in its environment.

The School. This familiarization with the temporal structures of the family in turn prepares the child for a further, more formal, encounter with organization; that is, for its time at school. It is here that the child experiences a more rigid temporal discipline: from the fixed lengths of daily and weekly attendance, to the formal separation of activities.[2] The school day is segmented into precise temporal units, with each unit devoted to a specific topic or task. The child learns that school has a primary claim on its time. It learns to accept the school's organization of time as legitimate — even when the school extends its temporal influence beyond its physical boundaries; as, for example, in the assignment of homework.

The Work-place. Above all, though, the formal times of the school prepare the individual for entering the organization demanding the greatest time-discipline of all — the work-place. Joining a modern work organization represents the final stage in conditioning the individual to an 'organized' time-consciousness.

While in chapter 2 we noted how in most primitive and developing economies work systems either are, or have been, primarily task-oriented, in modern industrialized economies they are time-oriented. In the factory or office employees are held to minimum temporal standards: their workday is characterized by known temporal parameters and constraints. Through the combination of minute specialization and fine measurement, industrial workers become subject not merely to temporal cycles based on the week, day or hour, but to ones defined by minutes or even seconds.[3]

ORGANIZATIONAL TIME

Our analysis begins to suggest three things: that time-sense is central to human life; that during maturation individuals become entrained to times regulated by their environment; and that through socialization individuals learn that temporal structuring is a major element in organizing. We are saying that while individuals experience time as natural and inherent, and while their subjective awareness of time becomes expressed in the construction of (inter-subjective) temporal meanings, nevertheless, in modern society pressures for synchronization force time-sense to become objectified and constrained. In order to be organized, individuals must subscribe to times which are rational but external. In administrative society, social (subjective-micro) times, which are regulated by the group, must operate within impersonal (objective-macro) times which are regulated by technology.

Externality and Specialization

We argue, therefore, that as societies become more complex, then work organizations become primitive claimants of time. In modern, industrial societies the formal, external organization has replaced the family as the main locus of time structuring. As the family has lost many of its functions to outside agencies, it has likewise relinquished claims on its members' time (Moore 1963a: 71ff).

Indeed, familial functions have been surrendered in line with greater specialization around distinct foreign agencies. Social functions have become the province of organizations such as the state, the factory, the shop, and the school. Notable here has been the externalization of child education, and the removal from the home of the main forms of economic production. In fact the only significant productive functions which remain are those of cooking, cleaning, child care, laundry, and shopping.

In the wake of this specialization, family members have now devoted their time to performing one particular role within a single place of work. Modern employment practice has demanded that we acquire expertise in one specific field. It demands that we develop skills relevant to a career. As individuals have exchanged utility for specialization, and therefore moved from the organic 'world we have lost' to the mechanistic 'world we now inherit' (Laslett 1965), so their worth has been checked on an external and generic social instrument — the career-ladder. Increasingly, success or failure is judged on one criterion — the timing of personal accomplishments.

The Career: Defining Status and Progress

It is the career which has become the dominant model for contemporary employment. As a concept it has become engrained into every day commonsense and culture. When western adults meet for the first time, the question they ask — 'What do you do?' — begs an answer that is singular, functional, and career-oriented; it begs an answer that is status-loaded and linear: an answer that can

85

be indexed directly to the wider social structure.

The notion of career is thus central to an assessment of the social position: it is the definer *par excellence* of the individual's progress in organized society; it is the central element in the list of social times which regulate biographies and determine personal worth.[4] Society determines a normative time chart for its members, and it is according to this chart that we construct appropriate timetables and schedules for living. So important are these timetables, that individuals no longer construct their biographies simply by passing through states determined by nature, but more importantly by reference to the sophisticated, normative structures of social life. An individual's biography is evaluated according to the rate and sequence with which he or she passes through what Glaser and Strauss (1965) term various 'status passages'; that is, through stages which relate the various positions and identities available in society.[5]

If we examine this idea more closely, we find that career is the concept which charts how individuals pass through a socially recognized and meaningful sequence of related events. As Hughes puts it, the career is 'the moving perspective in which the person sees his life as a whole and interprets the meaning of his various attributes, actions, and the things which happen to him' (Hughes 1971: 137). Through time, individuals develop a perspective in which their careers are endowed with particular meanings and values. As the person passes from one stage to another this perspective serves as a basis for assessment. Careers give the individual an acute sense of social time, and we think of ourselves in terms of a career path which includes the states of past, present, and future. As they pass from status to status, from organization to organization, individuals become sensitive to their relative position on the ladder of social biography. They ask whether they are living too rapidly or not rapidly enough? Is the pace of their biography concordant with the ideal? The career timetable is socially sanctioned and is based on a normative assessment of achievement. That is, it prescribes the normal time for a person to pass through these various stages. Any individual who is seen to progress at a rate faster or slower than normal risks being identified as an age deviate. Anyone who departs from age-related normalcy is likely to be attributed with having extraordinary skills, qualities, or characteristics.[6]

In modern societies, then, the relationship between age and career has become highly structured and formalized. Many organizations, starting with the school, provide detailed inventories which compare age with skill in order to arrive at selection. As work organizations become increasingly homogeneous, then the careers of a growing number of employees become interpreted in terms of age-grade relationships. Qualifications notwithstanding, an individual may simply be deemed too young or too old for higher office.[7]

SOCIAL TIME AND ORGANIZATIONAL TIME

Thus far, we have shown how human temporality is founded upon both natural and social imperatives. Although we have illustrated how our basic time-sense stems from physiological needs, we have noted also how our demands become entrained by the environment and structured by society. This brief analysis has shown how, in the course of human development, we increasingly structure our actions according to what we believe are 'proper' social times. Individuals acquire complex and detailed sets of temporal patterns based on practices they learn from their environment. While we discover that every day actions (e.g. manipulation and locomotion) have a temporal basis (e.g. in synchronization and sequence: see below), we note also how in enacting these skills, parameters are set in accordance with social order. We learn that for much behaviour cultural restrictions — notably concerning the 'correct' sequence of actions — override the natural dictates of the physiology and psychology of maturation (Gesell and Ilg 1943; Bruner 1960). Indeed, we note above all that 'beyond the bare physiological necessities for survival and such universal physiological attributes of the human species as standing erect and walking . . . the temporal order is a social order' (Moore 1963a: 44).[8]

However, while we have argued that the temporal order is a social order, and while we have noted that individuals acquire much of their time-sense in social organizations, we have not yet discussed the chief characteristics of this 'social' time.[9] We have not described the formal properties of social time, or asked why these are so central to the activities of organizations. Therefore, having considered developmental aspects of social time, we must now begin to introduce structural ones. In order to do this, we turn to writers who have developed formal typologies and models.

Wilbert Moore

In Chapter 2, we noted how Georges Gurvitch (1964) outlined eight

87

dimensions of social time.[10] However, we also noted that his works are opaque, and that his categories do not make for easy comprehension; nor for a clear analytical scheme. Indeed, faced with the difficulties in Gurvitch's work, writers seeking to develop models have tended to avoid his thesis and to turn instead to other, less varnished, sources. In this process, a source they have tapped more than any other has been the functionalist sociology of Wilbert Moore, and in particular the typology of times presented in *Man, Time and Society* (1963a).[11]

. Moore (1963a) suggests that as we move away from the physiology of co-ordinated acts and towards explicit social behaviour, then the proper timing of actions becomes a matter of response to social rules. His argument is summarized as follows: 'Social behaviour depends for its orderly qualities on common definitions, assumptions and actions with regard to the location of events in time. Certain activities, for example, require simultaneous action by a number of persons, or at least their presence at a particular time . . . Thus one element of temporal ordering is *synchronization*. Other activities require that actions follow one another in prescribed order; thus *sequence* is a part of the temporal order. For still other activities the frequency of events during a period of time is critical; thus *rate* also is one of the ways that time impinges on social behaviour. For all these elements of social behaviour *timing* is useful, since it denotes precisely the critical importance of some temporal order . . . If activities have no temporal order, they have no order at all' (Moore 1963a: 8–9).

Synchronization

If we expand Moore's three-fold classification, we find that by *synchronization* he and his followers refer to the adjustment of various social units with each other.[12] Lauer (1980), for example, notes how it is the need to synchronize activities which has led to the emphasis on clock-time in the modern world. With the increasing scope of communication and with the problem of interacting with a plurality of times, the need arises for a (single) time that will allow diverse groups to co-ordinate their actions.[13] The argument is made that without the benefit of either precise time measurement, or an independent source of 'standard time', the exact nature of synchronization can never be understood.

To support this argument, Moore and his followers offer a series of examples. One which is cited regularly concerns the use of direct sensory communication to secure synchronized actions and short-cycle rhythms. Moore outlines how audible and visible signals have long served to summon group members to related activities; and how they in fact still survive the invention of extremely accurate clocks. He notes for instance how the fitting of melodies to synchronized cadences is a special illustration of sophisticated responses to common sensory signals. Using the example of communication in the modern Navy, he suggests that, 'It would be a brave man who maintained that the electronic assistance of the public address system . . . represents an untarnished improvement over the sea chanteys that paced synchronized movements on sailing ships' (p. 46).[14]

Thus, synchronization is readily enacted where individual or intermittent activity is inadequate to accomplish tasks. Synchronization is crucial for the adjusting of two or more processes to each other so that their activities do not conflict. This is especially important when the multiplicity of activities that comprise a complex social situation must be co-ordinated so as to give appropriate scope for the operation of all (Lauer 1980). As Lewis and Weigart suggest, synchronicity 'works as a mechanism for making the rationality of human action and planning plausible' (1981: 451). Although for our present purposes it is the synchronization of the work-group which comes to mind, we must remember that close timing extends deep into the organization of life in general.[15]

Sequence

For his second element, sequence, Moore suggests that to be meaningful many activities require a correct ordering of their constituent actions. He argues that the sequential ordering of actions not only represents a 'priority schedule', but can also reflect a set of 'values'. For example, while the caution 'work before play' provides a rank order as well as a temporal order, it also implies a value hierarchy. Similarly, whereas in Christian tradition Sunday is regarded both as the first day of the week and — more importantly — the day of worship, in the secular view it is simply part of the week*end*. Thus, for many activities, Moore shows how their properties — and therefore their meaning — are threatened when we change the established order.

Moore also notes how norms of sequence apply at the seemingly mundane level of interpersonal communication. He notes that whereas the ordering of verbal exchange is a simple and straightforward phenomenon, the issue of who initiates a communication — and also of the degree of requiredness in reciprocation — can be one governed by a complex array of norms. Moore points to the priority given to high status communicators, and to the depth of meaning behind everyday euphemisms such as 'speaking out of turn'.

Rate

Moore's final temporal element is that of rate — what Zerubavel (1976) and Lauer (1980) call 'tempo'. This refers to the fact that when an order of events is to be encased within a stipulated period, then it must include an activity rate. This of course is the situation common in modern production systems, and especially in manufacturing (Clark *et al* 1984). The rule here is that while it is possible to use varied tempos to achieve standard output levels (e.g. by autonomous group working), in practice the very fact of deploying interdependent systems is usually enough to see rates subject to stringent and uniform control (e.g. in Fordism). Industrial engineers have long argued that action that is too fast or too slow will upset the other two elements of temporal ordering; i.e. synchronization and sequence. The axiom of post-Taylorist production systems has been to process work at a quick but constant tempo, the goal being to eliminate any temporal 'porosity' from the working period (Marx 1976, part 3; Clark *et al* 1984).

PART TWO: ORGANIZATIONS IN THEMSELVES

Thus far, we have described some of the natural and social imperatives of 'human-times'; explained how in modern society personal progress is assessed by 'career-times'; and introduced some of the formal characteristics of 'organized times'. As such, we have now completed our analysis at the micro level. We now turn to the time problems faced by organizations as entities in themselves. We shift the focus from ideographic concerns with experience to objective concerns with structuring.

TEMPORAL STRUCTURING

Uncertainty and Control

In Chapter 2 we suggested that given the dominant conception of time in our culture as scarce, valuable, homogeneous, linear, and divisible, and given the dominant characteristics of work organizations as functional, specialized, formalized, and rational, then organizations are confronted with three key-time problems: the reduction of temporal uncertainty; the resolution of conflicts over temporal activities; and the allocation of scarce temporal resources (McGrath and Rotchford 1983). However, in attempting to resolve these problems, we find also that three temporal issues emerge, all of which are related to the scheme outlined earlier by Moore (1963a). These are: the need for time schedules; i.e. for reliable predictions of the points in time at which specific actions will occur: the need for synchronization; i.e. for temporal co-ordination among functionally segmented parts and activities; and the need for time allocation; i.e. for distributing time so that activities will consume it in the most efficient and rational way.[16] In this section, we analyse the relationships between these various problems and issues.

For a structural analysis of temporal uncertainty, James Thompson's (1967) *Organizations in Action* represents a valuable first model (Clark 1982; McGrath and Rotchford 1983). In this work Thompson contrasts, albeit implicitly, problems of temporal structuring with those of organizational structuring. In focusing upon the changing nature of organizational environments, he brings out the difficulties encountered when organizations seek to establish stable and efficient time structures. Indeed, he not only illustrates problems stemming from temporal uncertainty, but also those which arise when applying generic solutions such as scheduling, synchronization and allocation.

In Thompson (1967) a central theme is that organizations have a technical core that requires protection against uncertainty. He suggests that to operate successfully, an organization needs to comprehend — and as far as possible control — the numerous environmental forces which impinge on its day-to-day activities. However, whereas this may seem a straightforward task for organizations operating in stable environments, he notes that for those operating in dynamic ones there is a need to protect the technical core through: 'buffering to absorb the uncertainty'; 'smoothing and levelling to reduce the amount of uncertainty'; and 'anticipating and adapting the environmental uncertainty so that it can be treated as a constant constraint within the organization functions'. It is these strategies, he argues, which make the interaction of organization and environment more predictable; i.e. because they reduce the uncertainty over the availability and timing of resources. In particular, it is these processes which illustrate the importance of efficient scheduling; for they suggest ways of resolving temporal uncertainty by increasing the predictability of when some event will occur and/or when some product will be available (McGrath and Rotchford 1983: 72).

Figure 8 Types of task interdependence in organization design

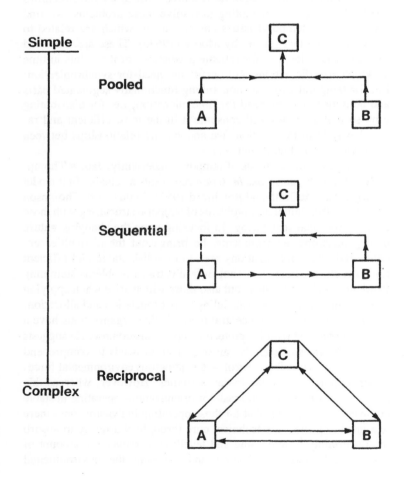

In developing this argument, Thompson (1967) outlines three types of intra-organizational interdependence, each of which, he suggests, requires a different type of co-ordination (see Figure 8). First, he talks of 'pooled interdependence', where all organization units contribute to and are supported by the organization as a whole, and where co-ordination is achieved by employing standardized units and regulations. Second, he discusses 'sequential interdependence', where the outputs of one unit form inputs to another, and where co-ordination is achieved through planning. And third, he talks of 'reciprocal interdependence', where the outputs of one unit are inputs to all other units, and where co-ordination is achieved through ongoing mutual adjustment among units. His argument here, is that for organizations to operate efficiently these three interdependencies must be co-ordinated rationally. To effect this, organizations must group units by type of interdependence into layers and departments. The purpose of such grouping is to minimize the costs associated with communication and decision-effort times. As such, groupings must be made first on the basis of reciprocally interdependent units, because they involve the greatest communication and decision/effort time. The second most time-costly to co-ordinate are sequentially interdependent units, so they have the next priority in hierarchical and departmental grouping. And, finally, as the pooled interdependent units are the least time-costly to co-ordinate, they are grouped only after the reciprocal and sequentially interdependent positions have been arranged (McGrath and Rotchford 1983).

Thompson suggests, therefore, that a major imperative in organizational structuring is the desire to minimize communication and decision/effort times. He argues that co-ordination through the standardized rules of pooled interdependence requires 'less frequent decisions and a smaller volume of communication during a specific period of operations than does planning, and planning calls for less decision and communication than does mutual adjustment' (p. 56). Through this analysis, we see that a major reason why decision and communication activities incur costs is that they consume time — they use up scarce temporal resources.[17]

Conflict over activities

For our second problem — conflict over activities — we consider how functionally segmented actions can be co-ordinated through specialization, and through interpersonal norms.

In dealing with the co-ordination of segmented activities, we are concerned with questions of synchronization rather than with scheduling. However, our sights are not so much set on what synchronization means at the level of the organization (i.e. a structural perspective), but more what it means for the individual (i.e. a process perspective). We are concerned with: (a) the temporal patterning of the individual's own multiple actions; (b) the temporal patterning of the individual's actions in relation to those of other individuals; and (c) the temporal patterning of the individual's actions in relation to other objects or events (e.g. the timing of a machine, the activities of another unit, etc.). The difference between the two perspectives, is that while for the organization such patterning is a problem only in respect to the efficient arranging of events, for individuals it points to a need to operate within an elaborate set of procedures and/or norms.[18]

As Max Weber described, the logic of organization is such that the larger and more complex an organization becomes, the greater functional specialization it will display. As functional specialization requires the synchronization of various parts and activities, the more need there is for temporal co-ordination of the various activities among the various parts. However, while the logic of specialization demands that each individual performs one function efficiently, this is at the cost of being able to perform a number of functions overall. As activities become more finely specified, and in turn as their location in a temporal pattern becomes more fixed, the more pressure there is to apply principles of formalization; or even to automate the whole activity. The irony here is that while the need for increased synchronization is a direct consequence of functional specialization, what is needed to accomplish this — i.e. the co-ordination of workers on individual tasks — violates one of the premises on which functional specialization is founded: the interchangeability of parts.[19]

Nevertheless, not all of an organization's activities are reducible to such tight specifications. Nor is all temporal organizing so mechanical. There indeed remain may organizational activities which require the synchronizing of individuals — as subjective actors — as well as of processes. While these activities require temporal co-ordination, this is achieved not so much by mechanistic specialization, but more by the organic process of developing implicit working norms.

Norms develop during interaction in order to help to synchronize the activities of participants. As failure to synchronize activities can be a major cost to both productive efficiency and group satisfaction, time-norms emerge in order to reduce such costs. As we move from dyadic interaction to the activities of larger groups, synchronization of norms becomes all the more important, because the temporal and spatial needs of such large, complex systems become more demanding. However, as in turn the criticality of such norms increases, then the greater the need becomes to make such norms explicit so they can be understood by all. Indeed, eventually implicit regulatory norms get translated into explicit rules, regulations and standard operating procedures, with these now formalized sets of expectations becoming associated with specific 'positions' or 'roles' in the organizational network. In the process of organizational growth, the norms by which actors regulate their actions become mere subsets of the role expectations extant in the formal organizational structure. No longer are behaviours indexed to particular individuals, groups, and situations, as they are objectified instead on to particular functions. It is the role which acts, not the actor. Positions which are formalized in the shape of recognized organizational procedures allow for expertise only within an established framework of regulations.[20] Normative procedures become control devices which operate in the service of smooth temporal co-ordination; that is, they effect explicit synchronization between the various activities of the organization's members (Clark 1982: 22; McGrath and Rotchford 1983: 84).

Scarcity

For the third problem, 'scarcity', we are concerned with matching productive activities to limited time allocations; that is, with 'the efficient assignment of temporal resources to tasks, hence the assignment of priorities or values to the tasks and assignment of responsibility for those tasks to staff' (McGrath and Rotchford 1983: 85). Our goals here are twofold: (at the macro level) to balance temporal resources between units; and (at the micro level) to obtain optimal matches between an employee's available time and the number of actions to be performed.[21]

While in the next section we discuss scarcity issues at the macro level, here we note some problems arising at the micro level. In particular we note how the matching of time and activities forms the basis for the employee's role/load problems — a form of stress which results from a perceived scarcity of time relative to the requirements of tasks to be performed. In the United States, a national study of workers undertaken by Kahn *et al* (1964) found that role overload was the single most pervasive form of stress in organizations. Role overload, it would seem, is now almost an inevitable consequence of the interaction between western time culture and modern forms of organization; that is, of the interaction of functional specialization, temporal and spatial segregation, synchronization, and fine time measurement. In modern societies, adults are likely to divide their time between many spatially, functionally, and temporally segregated organizations (e.g. in relation to work, the family, recreation, religion, etc.). As such, these sophisticated time allocations, and the temporal precision that comes with them, can become double-edged. While on the one hand this makes synchronization (within narrow time-tolerances) more feasible; on the other, the ability to account for increasingly precise time allocations gives individuals scope to pack activities more tightly into their roles. This can have the effect of increasing: the perceived scarcity of time in each role; the precision required for synchronizing between roles; and the strains on the boundaries between roles.

SOLVING TIME PROBLEMS IN ORGANIZATIONS

In this final section, we describe some of the tactics which organizations use to cope with time scarcity. In particular we examine three ways of coping with tight temporal constraints: by adjusting the specific time locations of activities; by redistributing peak-time loads over other phases of time cycles; and by trying to recover time that would otherwise be lost.

Altering Time Locations

For the first of the tactics, adjusting the specific time locations of activities, we refer to instances in which organizations need ways of freeing activities from their fixed locations in 'real' time. For example, the most pressing time problem for employees is the pressure to do two or more things simultaneously (or in other words, the pressure imposed by multiple, conflicting demands either within one role or across two or more roles). The only solution to this problem is through time relocation: through having one or more of these events extracted from its location and rescheduled.

While some events are relatively amenable to temporal relocations, and can easily be extracted from context — i.e. processes which can be easily separated from related processes — others cannot be so readily extracted, and depend instead on being enacted at a specific place and at a specific time (as, for example, two incompatible uses of a shop display during Christmas week, or two incompatible uses of a religious site on a holy day). However, while such temporal conflicts are not easily remedied, and while such problems must generally be solved by assigning priorities, nevertheless, in recent years certain technological developments have given partial solutions. Video-taping, for example, has meant that we can record certain activities (e.g. meetings, events) in real time and then react to them when convenient. This enables rescheduling, whereas previously the only viable solution would have been through prioritizing.

Other real-time problems occur when events happen either too fast to be comprehended or too slowly to be observed effectively. For example, a detailed conversation may occur at such a high speed that it is impossible to decipher in real time. On the other hand, a meeting may take longer than we wish to spend on it. Here, means are required for altering the duration of a given event; or, more correctly, for altering the rate at which the event took place. Once again, some of these problems have been resolved by technological developments. Audio recordings, for example, can be played at a substantially faster rate without great distortions in frequency. This permits the listener to comprehend the material more quickly than it occurred in real time. Similarly, many tape recorders have functions for slowing speech in order to make it more comprehensible. These are all techniques for controlling the rate at which certain activities occur. They decouple the activities from the rate at which they occurred in nature to a rate (faster or slower) that is more effective for the purposes of the individuals concerned. They allow a better fit between the amount of time necessary to effect certain activities and the amount of time available to manage them.

Yet another, related problem concerns the need for parts of activities to be accomplished in a fixed, temporally-co-ordinated sequence. As work activities tend to be structured linearly, so that the sequence covers a substantial period of real time, this can be problematic in two ways: (a) because the total time required may not allow the task sequence to be accomplished quickly enough (i.e. to meet a deadline); or (b) because the individual may not be able to commit sufficient time, at a given time, to effect the whole process. For these situations, methods are required for uncoupling the sequence-linkages between sub-stages of the task, so that constituent sub-tasks can be accomplished in temporal isolation.

For the first problem, large tasks are often subdivided into sub-stages which are then executed in temporal parallel. Although this does not save time, in the sense of the staff hours used, it serves to get the whole task completed sooner in real-time, even though a price may be paid in terms of the detailed co-ordination of the separately executed parts. Similarly, for the latter problem, a large task may be divided into several small segments that can be accomplished over a wide stretch of real time. For example, when prioritizing tasks, organizations often arrange for certain jobs to be accomplished only when no urgent work is at hand; e.g. maintenance, safety, and renovation.[22]

Distributing Time Loads

For the second coping strategy, redistributing peak-time loads, we are concerned here with the re-allocation of activities in order to make better use of the system capacity as a whole. In other words, to operate more effectively by either increasing capacity during periods of low load or increasing capability during periods of high load.

In practice, the former often involves experiments in 'inverse-pricing' — that is, in attempts to encourage demand during unfashionable, low-load periods of reduced unit prices. Common methods for accomplishing this are, for example, offering 'off-peak' rates for electricity, telephones, transport, and advertising; 'off-season' rates for holidays and flights; and 'end-of-season' prices for clothes, sporting equipment, etc.[23]

During periods of high demand, organizations simply provide more capability, notably by getting more staff-hours devoted to peak-load activities. Recently, however, and as markets have become more volatile, organizations have started to balance loads by distinguishing between core and peripheral workforces, again so as to buffer against uncertainty. In order to balance staff demands with market demands, organizations have recruited a greater percentage of employees on short, fixed-term contracts — contracts with little protection under employment legislation. Similarly, because firms wish to keep labour costs to a minimum, recent decades have seen a growth in agencies supplying temporary, predominantly female, labour for generic tasks at short notice — a practice commonly referred to as 'temping'.

Reclaiming Time

The techniques above are all strategies for avoiding time waste in work systems. However, despite our desires to eliminate such waste, the very logic of modern organization — i.e. functional specialization and temporal segregation — means that certain pieces of time are inevitably lost. As specialization and segregation encourage planning in ever more precise temporal divisions, so the very fact of slicing work into smaller intervals means that slivers of time are lost in the process. The reclamation of time lost in such transitions remains one of the major areas for increasing the efficiency of production systems.

Other arenas of 'wasted' time are those of travelling and waiting. While in one sense these sections of time are filled, in that they are dedicated to specific purposes, to most of us they represent intervals which are empty. As such, they are time-spaces open to development. Many commuters for instance try to use up travelling time by writing reports, dictating letters, or simply reading work-related literature. For others, travelling to work now represents an opportunity to conduct business with the office or with customers direct, e.g. through the use of car phones.

Finally, and related to the above, is the double use of time that is not filled with waiting, but with activity. By this, we mean that time can be saved by the purposeful combining of activities which, while different in nature, can be oriented towards the same productive goal. Examples of these are the working lunch and the executive golf game. Both are designed to help business dealings by making the interaction between the parties less formal and more enjoyable. In both cases the objective is to mesh the performance of two roles efficiently and effectively.

CONCLUSION

In this chapter, we have analysed the complex relationship between time and organization. In so doing, we have assessed not only the natural imperatives underpinning this relationship, but also the social ones. We have argued that although natural-times remain potent in our organizing, these become regulated by social-times. We have suggested, that as personal development is joined by social development, then we appreciate time as a vehicle which brings us within the orbit of human affairs.

As we enter the world of affairs, we find that a major function of socialization is the structuring of our time-sense within formal institutions. Notable here is the process whereby school and workplace teach us rigid time disciplines. They segment activities into precise temporal units, and condition us to an 'organized' time-consciousness. This conditioning sees us subscribe to times which are external and specialized — times which are technocratic. Indeed, in the west, the external and highly specialized organization has become not only the main regulator of social time, but also its primary claimant.

In organized society, we structure our actions according to what we feel are 'proper' social times. We base our temporal understanding on practices we learn from the environment. In dealing with sophisticated social structures, we develop ways of expressing our needs for co-ordinated acts. To reproduce order, we create common definitions and assumptions in regard to the location of events in time. In particular, we form common understandings of synchronization, sequence, and rate. Given the increasing scope of human communication — and thus the problem of dealing with a plurality of times — we seek understandings that allow diverse groups to adjust their actions mutually: we require general temporal agreements so that we can relate processes in ways which avoid their activities becoming conflictual. This is especially necessary in situations where actions must be regulated in order to give scope for each to fulfil its potential.

Temporal structuring is thus at the heart of organization. When organizations are designed or changed, then temporal factors are of primary concern. As the logic of organization is that with increased size comes greater specialization, then time emerges as a central feature of structuring. Time is basic to resolving problems of environmental uncertainty, conflicts over activities, and the allocation of scarce resources. Synchronization, sequence, and rate are all crucial when we seek predictions when specific actions will occur relative to others; when we attempt to co-ordinate functionally segmented parts and activities; and we want to distribute time so that activities consume it in the most efficient manner. In competitive markets, organizations are driven to find new ways of reducing communication and decision-effort times. They seek new techniques for reducing levels of conflict between activities, and in particular of effecting superior co-ordination by developing more sophisticated specialization and more appropriate normative values.

100

NOTES

1. That is, 'circadian' from the Latin *circa*, about; and *dies*, day.

2. Lewis and Weigart (1981) note how even before the child enters kindergarten it is likely to have experienced the bureaucratic timetables of a pre-school day-centre or nursery. They note how these institutions possess well-established criteria of efficiency and standardization, and relatively clear markers of progress.

3. Such temporal specialization does not, however, end with assembly-line operatives. Demands for parts and storage are closely linked to the temporal demands of the work pace. Thus in many factories the tempo of the productive process impinges on a large proportion of the workforce. This is especially true in factories adopting the Japanese inventory control system of 'just-in-time' production (see Schonberger 1982).

4. For example, it is society which specifies when it is time for us to vote, drink alcohol, drive a car, marry, go to school, retire, etc. (Lewis and Weigart 1981: 443).

5. As Lewis and Weigart (1981) note, the availability of such positions and identities is influenced by factors such as age, sex, race, and class.

6. The question of the rate of career progression is one which anticipates political behaviour within organizations. A regular complaint within organizations is that many employees expend too much of their energy on political objectives — and especially on in-fighting — and not enough on work objectives. To keep ahead of the 'biological clock', employees, driven by a belief in zero-sum advancement, spend time devising political strategies to scupper the aspirations of peers (Swingle 1976). Indeed, the spectre that haunts middle managers is of time standing still; of being amongst those who become 'over-age' for promotion and thus who find themselves frozen in their position. Perhaps the one who is asked to resign prematurely; or the one who becomes out of line with the demography of the work-place, and who then feels obliged to look for work that will re-align him with his biography (Moore 1963a).

7. Of course, securing advancement is not simply a function of possessing appropriate levels of knowledge and skill — many exogenous factors affect this relationship. Differences in the fortunes of occupational sectors may mean that an individual working in an expanding field may advance far more rapidly than a counterpart of equal or greater competence in a less dynamic one. Similarly, for workers employed within the same organization, changes in the market demand for certain skills may witness great differences in the promotion rates of individuals whose abilities and ambitions are to all intents and purposes similar.

8. Moore could perhaps express this argument better. While factors such as standing erect and walking are indeed what Winch (1958) would call 'biological universals', Moore fails to note how these factors can also be 'social'; that is, they have the capacity to be styled and moulded through social interaction; their enactment can take the form of intentional behaviour.

9. As the temporal order becomes such a social order, then common assumptions/definitions about the nature of time develop. The social nature of time means that we create, as Zerubavel (1976) puts it, 'standard times'

for interpreting the nature of formal organization. This argument maintains that: 'A standard time-orientation, consisting of standard units of duration and a standard system of time-reference, is a basic prerequisite for participation in the social world' (Zerubavel 1976: 88).

10. The times listed by Gurvitch are: 'enduring' time — time slowed down, of long duration; 'deceptive' time — sharp crises that produce a time of surprises; 'erratic' time — time of irregular pulsation; 'cycle' time — past, present, and future revolve in a cycle; 'retarded' time — time too long awaited; 'alternating' time — time of delay and advance; 'time pushing forward' — future becomes the present; and 'explosive' time — time of creation.

11. Notable amongst those influenced by Moore are Heirich (1964), who identifies social time as a 'social factor', a 'causal link', a 'quantitative measure', and a 'qualitative measure'; Zerubavel (1976), who lists 'duration', 'sequence', 'timing', and 'tempo' as 'the fundamental structural dimensions of social time'; Lauer (1980), who suggests that there are 'five basic elements in the temporal pattern of any social phenomenon' — 'periodicity', 'tempo', 'timing', 'duration', and 'sequence'; and Lewis and Weigart (1981), who argue that there are 'three basic features of social times' — 'embeddedness', 'stratification', and 'synchronization'. While these latter accounts all are well crafted, they make few advances on Moore's (1963a) account.

12. See Lewis and Weigart on 'synchronicity' (1981: 451) and the sections on 'timing' in Zerubavel (1976: 89) and Lauer (1980: 32).

13. Hence the emergence of the quantitative, homogenous, infinitely divisible time of classical mechanics (see Chapter 2).

14. Moore gives many other examples of synchronized actions in organizations. For example, 'the cadence of hauling a fishnet to a boat or to shore, for moving a gigantic stone for building a pyramid, or pulling the oars of an ancient galley is matched by an orchestral conductor, or the sharp demands of the coxswain of a racing shell' (1963a: 46).

15. Lauer (1980) notes how synchronization is a crucial factor for issues as diverse as the initiation of planned social change, love-making, and the teaching of disturbed children.

16. The ways in which these three factors cause specific problems for organizations are neatly summarized by McGrath and Rotchford: 'The function of scheduling is prediction, which involves resolution of the problem of temporal uncertainty. The function of synchronization is co-ordination in time, which also involves reduction of temporal uncertainty and is likely to involve resolution of conflicts of interest amongst parts of the organization. The function of allocation is the distribution of scarce (temporal) resources, which involves resolution of conflicting claims on those scarce resources and also involves resolution of the problem of the inherent scarcity of time' (1983: 71).

17. To reproduce order, organizations demand tight control over the present and a degree of certainty about the future. In sectors where change is a problem, firms allocate a large percentage of their resources to the anticipation of future demands. When faced with turbulent markets, firms build redundancy into their systems ('organizational slack'); they champion departments whose main role is the detection of threats and opportunities in the environment (e.g. marketing, corporate planning, credit control, R and D: see Emery and Trist 1965: Roeber 1973; Miles 1980).

18. While time is a major concern for organizational planning, it is also important for the here and now of production and administration. Large firms are obliged to estimate the time required to complete accepted orders and, on this basis, to anticipate timetables for future projects. When resources are allocated based on these predictions, departments are under pressure to comply with these schedules. As manufacturing firms organize production according to a fixed sequence of phases, if one takes too long it subsequently disrupts the timing of the remaining phases. The same is true for administrative acts. To be efficient, the complex control networks of administration depend on constantly fulfilling expectations regarding sequence and speed. As Moore suggests: 'The message that arrives "too soon", or more probably "too late", may be worse than simply disorderly; it may be disastrous' (1963a: 94). He notes how this is especially true in public bureaucracies, where massive and complex interdependences makes them ill-suited to accommodate alterations of course and procedure.

19. Problems of administrative communication and flexibility are inextricably linked to the problem of productive flexibility noted earlier. Once again the crucial issue is that of the balance between centralization and decentralization. Administrative decentralization, which truncates channels of communication by allowing decision-making at levels closer to those at which problems occur, also reduces the time-loss of reaction. In contrast, if problem-solving is retained exclusively at executive levels, then the only way to retain structural responsiveness is to speed-up the transmission of crucial, current-state information from the function, level, or unit responsible for its collection and evaluation; i.e. somehow to increase the pace of information supply to problem sites. However, the massive flow of communications in large bureaucratic organizations may so completely absorb an administrator's time that the result is that they lose all initiative, their actions becoming 'rule-bound' and 'mechanical' (Moore 1963a). Such tendencies have been documented in the literature which has studied, to use Merton's (1940) phrase, the 'dysfunctions of bureaucracy' (also Selznick 1949; Parsons 1937; Gouldner 1955; and Jacques 1976).

20. Further problems arise when production and administration operate in different time sequences; that is, when production is continuous while administration is discontinuous. Plants that manufacture on a 24-hour basis present the problem of providing supervisory, technical and managerial facilities for the 'unsocial' shifts. A similar problem faces multinational firms, or firms operating in worldwide markets but which require constant and rapid information flows (e.g. financial or commodity houses). Technological developments have no answer to the basic fact that clocks are set to different standard times. Important events in London may occur at times when New York and Tokyo are sleeping. Information requiring an administrative decision may not reach decision-makers during their normal decision-making time.

21. As one of the axioms of modern administration is that 'structure follows strategy', then the way organizations view the future determines how they deploy resources. For example, large bureaucracies have adopted rigid structures because they perceive the future as stable and certain. As the environment is felt to pose few threats, they feel confident with systems which are low on responsiveness. As adaptation is not a major issue, decision-making can be highly centralized and control procedures highly formalized. In

103

post- Second World War manufacturing, the relative stability of markets meant that for long periods (e.g. 1945–70) large-batch or mass production firms adopted highly centralized decision processes and highly formalized control systems. In growing but relatively stable markets these characteristics were optimal. This tradition, however, now stands in transition. Many modern manufacturers express desires to be innovative and thus to be 'change masters' (Kanter 1984). Currently, many modern firms are implementing cellular manufacturing systems in which small batches are produced efficiently. Such systems are seen to have many advantages, and especially that: set-up times and lag-times are reduced; capital tied up in the non-value added operations is reclaimed; and customer requirements are met quickly. As noted previously, the goal for many of these firms is producing goods the Japanese way, 'just-in-time'.

22. Industrial contractors sometimes offer reduced rates for work which can be accomplished at discretion; i.e. over a longer time period than normal. The advantage is that such arrangements allow the work to be completed in time slots that might otherwise have been wasted. These contracts act as buffers against uncertainties such as cancelled appointments, technical failures, bad weather, illness, etc.

23. Some other examples of organizations using non-peak time profitably are of churches being used during weekdays for civic activities, and schools/universities/colleges being used for evening classes or as conference centres.

6

Time and labour relations

Paul Blyton

INTRODUCTION

Together with wages, the length of the working period has represented a central issue in the development of industrial relations. In industrial society, labour has typically been purchased in temporal units (hours, days, weeks), establishing time rather than task as the primary concern in the wage-effort bargain. At the individual level, working-time has been altered not only by an irregular though persistent reduction in the length of the working week but also more recently by changes in the working year (through increased holiday entitlement) and the working lifetime (by later entry into the labour market, and the increased provision of early retirement schemes). The growth of unemployment has also reduced the total worktime of a significant minority within the labour force. At a more aggregate level, the total volume and distribution of worked time has been affected by the substantial increase in part-time working, to the point where in Britain more than one worker in five is now employed part-time.

In charting the patterns and changes in working-time, we can identify a number of roles which trade unions have played — for example in negotiating changes in hours, holidays, and retirement provision, and in administering the distribution of overtime and short-time working. In addition to this continued involvement in questions of duration, local union organizations have also played an important part in determining the intensity of work time, through, for example, the establishment of periodic breaks and agreements over work pace. As we shall see, in recent years the organization of worktime has become increasingly prominent within industrial relations, reflecting part of a broader management search for greater manpower 'flexibility'. In the 1970s, working-time flexibility was primarily associated with employees' flexibility in relation to their start, stop, and break times. In the 1980s, however, flexibility has come to be associated much more with employers' desire to reduce labour costs and increase productivity, partly by re-organizing working time to match operational demands and by reducing the amount of time spent at work but not actually working.

In tracing this growing management interest in more flexible worktime arrangements, similarities can be drawn with earlier experiences with productivity bargaining, one objective of which was the more efficient utilization of normal work hours (Flanders 1964). As with the conflicts arising over productivity bargaining, however, the recent search for a more 'flexible' approach to working-time and the attempted linking of negotiations over reduced hours with questions of the organization of worktime, has led to considerable disagreement and protracted negotiations between management and unions in Britain and abroad — for example in the flexible rostering dispute on the railways, the BL 'washing up' dispute, the 1987 Telecom strike, six-day working and longer shifts in the coal industry, and the negotiations over working-time changes in the British and German engineering industries.

While employers have focused increasingly on the issue of flexibility and the productive use of working-time, parts of the trade union movement, particularly in the late 1970s and early 1980s, expressed considerable interest in the reduction and re-organization of working-time as a means of creating jobs and reducing unemployment. This 'work-sharing' debate attracted much support and criticism both in Britain and abroad (Blyton 1982, 1987; Hinrichs et al 1985). The support for work-sharing lost momentum when it was demonstrated that reduced hours tended to be compensated by increased productivity rather than additional jobs (White 1982). However, as we will examine more closely below, some recent evidence from the West German engineering industry suggests a stronger work-sharing potential may exist after the scope for increased productivity has been exhausted.

Before examining these recent developments, however, it is necessary to establish their broader context by reviewing briefly the historical development of union involvement in working-time issues, and the general trends in the pattern of working-time. Among other things, this reveals how the earlier industrial relations focus on duration has given way more recently to the greater attention being paid to the internal organization of working-time.

106

THE PERIOD UP TO 1900

The development of industrialism was accompanied by changes in time discipline, with the emerging factory regime engendering a greater regularity in worktime, breaking down pre-industrial traditions of variation in work pace and duration (Thompson 1967; Blyton 1989b). This transition away from bouts of inactivity followed by long hours of arduous work had begun before the industrial revolution. Urban and commercial growth, a Puritan and later Methodist value on hard work and the condemnation of wasted time, coupled with developments in clock technology meant that for those living in towns at least, awareness of clock-time was already growing (though by no means complete) in the seventeenth and eighteenth centuries, if not before (Thrift 1981; Harrison 1986). Rural labour, however, was less measured by the clock than by the amount of daylight and urgency of tasks; hours were long but as in cottage industry, there was a measure of variety and 'porosity' in the working day.

This pre-industrial irregularity did not cease with the onset of industrialization. On the contrary, for several decades traditional work rhythms vied with those which factory owners sought to impose (Thompson 1967). The continued widespread adherence to 'Saint' Monday (taking Monday as a second rest day, following Sunday), and the considerable employer criticism voiced against worker irregularity reflected a period when rural labour was migrating in large numbers into nearby towns, when small workshops with more traditional notions of time-discipline still predominated over large factories, and when workers were not as yet fully responsive to their employer's financial penalties and inducements to regularity, but rather retained a stronger value towards free time once subsistence wages had been earned (Pollard 1963: 254). It was to be well into the nineteenth century before the factory was a bigger employer than the workshop and the employees' value system had altered to reflect a more aspiring and consumer-oriented outlook as more and more goods became available from the new factories and via improved transportation, and as real wages gradually rose to make the satisfaction of that consumer demand a greater possibility.

In Britain, the adjustment to a work routine which sought to enforce discipline and regularity (a discipline made more onerous by the monotony of mechanized work) occasioned a degree of collective as well as individual resistance — particularly on the part of skilled workers reacting to the undermining of their traditional basis of job control through the introduction of 'self acting' machines. However,

107

it was the specific issue of time duration — primarily the length of the working-day and week, and the related issue of compulsory overtime — which acted as a more explicit rallying point for trade unionism. Earlier in the century, the length of the working day in the textile industry had given rise to a prolonged campaign (the Ten Hours Movement), in which prominent politicians and businessmen such as Oastler, Sadler and Ashley (later the Earl of Shaftesbury) joined with grass roots Short-Time Committees to lobby for a ten-hour working day for women and children. After earlier (unenforced) legislation in 1802 and 1819, and some provision for shorter hours in the Factory Acts of 1833 and 1844, the Ten Hours Act was eventually passed in 1847, though even then employers soon managed to amend the Act to extend the hours of women and juveniles up to ten-and-a-half hours. Nevertheless, the 1847 Act laid the basis for limiting female and young people's work hours and was gradually extended to other industries by subsequent legislation. This nineteenth century legislation, however, referred only to women and children and excluded adult men.

Shortly after the Ten Hours Act, the Amalgamated Society of Engineers (ASE) was established to further the skilled workers' objectives of eliminating unemployment in the engineering industry, resisting the flood of unskilled labour and restoring the bargaining power of the skilled men. To this end the Society focused its attention on piece-work and systematic overtime, both of which were seen to undermine the craftsmen's bargaining position. Overtime working had grown over the previous generation as a result of the increase in capital investment and employers' desire to maximize utilization of the new machinery. Opposition to systematic overtime was written into the ASE rule book and became 'a crucial part of ASE policy' (Burgess 1975: 18). It also became one of the points of contention in the first major dispute in which the embryonic union was involved — a five-month lock-out which resulted in defeat for the union and evidenced the weak bargaining position of skilled workers in the face of employer opposition, technological change, and widespread introduction of unskilled labour to man the new machines (Burgess 1975: 23–4).

Around this time too, a Nine Hours Movement became active though it was not until the early 1870s, when the economy was buoyant and labour-power strengthened by low unemployment, that hours declined. By 1875, however, the 54-hour week was becoming widespread. The shorter Saturday had also been established (or probably, re-established since the Saturday half-day was apparently common in the early medieval period; see Bienefeld 1972). This began a process of defining what we now think of as the non-working weekend, and undermined the tradition among higher paid artisans of treating Monday as an additional rest day (Reid 1976).

In Britain, the formal length of the working week remained virtually unaltered until the end of the First World War, though this masks pressure by employers to extend it (which they were able to do through compulsory overtime) and by unions to reduce it. This union pressure was concentrated in a campaign in the late 1880s and 1890s to establish an eight-hour working day. This demand had earlier been adopted by the International Workingmen's Association (the First International) in the 1860s, but found concerted support in Britain in the unskilled unions which began forming in the late 1880s. Prominent spokesmen in favour of an eight-hour day included Tom Mann and Sidney Webb (Mann 1967; Webb and Cox 1891; also, Harris 1972). Yet for a variety of reasons the Eight Hours Movement was unsuccessful at this time. For a start, the trade unions were divided on strategy, with the unskilled unions (and after 1890, the TUC) tending to favour a legislative approach similar to their Ten Hours counterparts half a century earlier, while the more established craft unions generally advocated a reduction of hours through collective bargaining or 'conciliation'. This lack of unanimity was exacerbated by the responses of prominent employers to a shorter day. An important plank in the union platform for an eight-hour day was the argument that unemployment would be reduced by the work-sharing effect which shorter hours would generate (see for example Webb and Cox 1891: 107). In the event, however, a number of employer publications (such as by the owner of the Sheffield steel firm Hadfield's) argued that in plants where hours had been reduced to eight, no extra employment had been created and the time lost by the reduction had been offset by less fatigue and greater productivity (Hadfield and Gibbins 1892). Thus, by the mid 1890s the Eight Hours Movement in Britain had lost considerable momentum; the question of hours was not to become prominent again until after the First World War.

Despite the reductions in the third quarter, by the end of the nineteenth century working hours were still long by today's standards and made more so by the widespread use of overtime and in some occupations (such as iron-making) the continuation of twelve-hour shifts. The lack of holidays added to the length and regularity of the working year. Bank Holiday Acts in 1871 and 1875 had introduced four days' statutory holiday but by the turn of the century paid holidays remained a rarity.

THE TWENTIETH CENTURY

Weekly Hours

In Britain, twentieth century changes in work hours have been concentrated into four short periods — immediately after the First and Second World Wars, the early 1960s and the late 1970s/early 80s. In general, these periods saw the introduction of the 48, 44, 40 and 39-hour normal workweek for manual workers (Blyton 1985: 22). These reductions tend to coincide with periods of rising real earnings (Bienefeld, 1972); the first two can also be linked to increased postwar expectations and the greater availability of skilled workers following demobilization.

Outside Britain, hours have also declined significantly during the twentieth century though different countries display considerable variation in the pace and timing of changes. In the United States, for example, hours fell considerably in the depression years of the early 1930s.[1] In 1929, average hours stood at just under fifty, but by 1940 this figure had declined to forty-two (Patten 1986). By 1950 average weekly hours in the United States had fallen further to stand at just above forty — a reduction of more than sixteen hours over the previous forty years (Patten 1986: 48; see also Owen 1979). This decline by 1940 was brought about partly by the Fair Labor Standards Act 1938, which required premium rates (time and a half) to be paid to certain groups beyond forty hours. The forty-hour average workweek represented a significantly lower level of hours than prevailed in Europe at that time, and helps to explain why hours changed little in the US over the succeeding forty years.

In Europe, the forty-eight hour week (excluding overtime) represented the general standard after the First World War; this fell to a basic workweek of forty-four hours in the years after the Second World War[2] (though a lower basic week of 40–2 hours existed in France, Australasia, and North America by this time). By the mid 1970s, a forty-hour basic workweek had been widely achieved, with several countries — Austria, Belgium and Scandinavia among them — introducing the reduction in a series of stages. Reductions were achieved via legislation and/or collective bargaining; some legislation on maximum hours exists in most industrial countries (Denmark and the UK are exceptions) though bargained agreements have in many cases brought actual hours considerably lower than legal maxima (Blyton 1989a).

Outside Europe and North America, the country whose hours have shown most variance with the general pattern outlined above is Japan. Working hours have tended to be longer in Japan than elsewhere, sustained partly by continued labour shortages in periods of rapid economic growth and partly due to a lack of priority among trade unions to press for reduced hours (Kotaro 1980: 71–2). This picture changed somewhat in the 1960s and early 70s, with the widespread adherence to a forty-two hour week by the early 1970s (Evans 1975; Blyton 1985: 30). Nevertheless, over the past decade average hours (including overtime) have actually slightly increased in Japan, following two decades of a declining trend (Shimada and Hayami 1986; see also Table 2 below). The tendency for Japanese workers to work almost half of their holiday entitlement has acted to maintain a higher-than-average level of annual hours (holiday entitlement is discussed separately in a later section). In non-capitalist countries, a working week of less than forty-five hours was adopted relatively early and in the USSR, forty-one hours represented the basic working week by 1960 (Solovyov 1962). International Labour Organization (ILO) data suggests relatively little change since that time, though in other Eastern bloc countries the standard work week appears somewhat longer (42–6 hours) than in the USSR.

Recent Developments in Working Hours

In the late 1970s and early 80s, many industrial countries experienced a further reduction in working time. In Table 2 only Japan evidences a rise in average annual hours between 1975 and 1985, though in the US the fall in hours is very small.

In France, legislation in 1981 (effective from 1982) reduced the statutory work week from forty to thirty-nine hours. In other countries, reductions were achieved through collective agreements, in some cases after lengthy disputes. In Britain (where more than seven million manual workers experienced a reduction in basic hours in the period 1980–3), the largest group involved in the reduction were engineering workers, who agreed a thirty-nine hour basic week (down from forty hours) following a series of overtime bans, and one and two day stoppages over a ten-week period in 1979. In West Germany, the dispute over working time in the engineering industry was much more dramatic: a demand by IG Metall for a thirty-five hour week led in 1984 to the largest strike in West German history. Agreement was eventually reached involving the introduction of an average 38.5-hour

111

Table 2 Average annual hours worked per person in employment[1] (1975 = 100)

	1975	1976	1977	1978	1979	1980	1981	1982	1983	1984	1985
Canada	100.0	99.5	97.7	98.3	97.7	97.1	96.1	94.7	94.1	94.5	95.0
Finland	100.0	99.5	99.2	99.3	98.2	97.0	96.7	95.7	94.8	94.2	—
France	100.0	100.2	98.6	98.0	98.2	98.5	97.1	92.7	91.5	—	—
Germany	100.0	101.9	100.3	98.6	97.8	97.2	96.3	96.6	96.2	95.8	94.5
Japan	100.0	101.3	101.4	101.7	102.3	102.0	101.6	101.4	101.5	102.4	—
Italy	100.0	99.9	98.0	97.5	97.2	97.2	96.9	96.5	95.8	95.0	94.3
Netherlands	100.0	100.5	99.2	96.8	94.4	94.5	94.7	95.1	94.6	92.2	—
Norway	100.0	97.8	95.6	94.4	93.4	93.3	92.1	92.1	91.6	90.8	91.4
Sweden	100.0	100.6	98.9	96.4	95.7	94.9	94.4	95.3	95.8	96.0	—
United Kingdom	100.0	99.1	98.1	97.0	96.5	94.1	91.1	91.9	91.2	92.0	—
United States	100.0	100.1	100.0	99.7	99.6	98.7	98.4	97.9	97.4	96.8	99.3

Source: Organisation for Economic Co-operation and Development (1986) *Employment Outlook*, Paris: OECD, p. 142.
1 These data refer, as far as possible, to the total economy, except in:
Japan: employees in enterprises with 30 or more employees.
Netherlands: persons employed in the private enterprise sector excluding agriculture and fishing.
United States: employees only.

week in the engineering, printing, and furniture industries, though the means of implementing this reduction was left to local agreement and gave significant scope for employers to introduce variation in weekly hours to meet market fluctuations (Bosch 1986b: 280).

These claims for shorter hours in the late 70s and early 80s were partly justified by trade unions in terms of their potential work-sharing effect, the reduced volume of hours worked being foreseen as creating additional employment opportunities. This support for work-sharing developed as unemployment increased in the 1970s; in 1979 the European Trade Union Confederation focused individual trade union calls for work-sharing by resolving in favour of a 10 per cent cut in working time (ETUI 1979). The EEC in a Draft Recommendation on the Reduction and Reorganization of Working Time in 1983 also identified positive employment effects from a cut in hours. During the 1980s, however, support for work-sharing lost much of its earlier momentum. As well as continued resistance to the work-sharing idea by most employers and many governments, the results of actual hours reduction showed little positive employment effect. In the case of the British engineering industry, for example, White and Ghobadian (1984) found that reductions had been offset by increased overtime and higher productivity resulting from changes in technology and work pace; increased employment resulting from the reduction in hours was negligible. The employment effects of time reductions in France and Belgium were similarly disappointing from the point of view of job creation (Blyton 1987). However, some recent evidence from the reduction in hours in the West German engineering industry suggests that the work-sharing potential of hours cuts may indeed be significant where available opportunities to rationalize production and increase productivity have already been taken (Bosch 1986b: 286–7).

Most recently, there have been further small reductions in working-time, as some work groups catch up with the earlier gains made by others. In Britain the average basic working week was thirty-nine hours for male manual workers in 1986, and thirty-seven hours for non-manual grades. In 1986 only about 15 per cent of manual employees in Britain worked a basic week of forty hours or more, while approximately 10 per cent had basic weekly hours of less than thirty-nine hours. The manual–non-manual discrepancy is evident for both males and females; in both sexes, overtime working widens this gap.

This manual–non-manual difference is also widespread abroad, though there are exceptions; in the Federal Republic of Germany, for example, manual workers achieved a forty-hour week earlier than

than their white-collar counterparts (Evans 1969: 40). Elsewhere the issue of harmonizing manual and non-manual conditions has become more prominent in recent years (Roberts 1985) though variations in hours appear to have declined less than some other inequities such as provisions for sickness pay and occupational pensions.

Overtime

Though in Britain trade union resistance to compulsory overtime dates back more than a century (see above), overtime has continued to represent a prominent part of working-time patterns in this and many other countries. Overtime — time worked in excess of 'standard' hours — is worked primarily by prime-age male manual workers in the manufacturing, transport, and communications sectors. In mid-1987 approximately 36 per cent of male manual workers in manufacturing worked an average of 9.4 hours' overtime per week. As basic hours have fallen for manual workers in Britain over the past two decades, the level of overtime has remained relatively high and over the postwar period as a whole has shown some tendency to increase (Bosworth and Dawkins 1981).

However, as Table 3 shows, since the mid-1960s the total number of overtime hours worked has fallen back due to the contraction of employment in manufacturing industries. In Europe, relatively high levels of overtime are also worked in France and the Republic of Ireland, whilst the Benelux countries and Denmark maintain comparatively low levels of overtime working partly due to legislative restrictions (ETUI 1979: 49; ILO 1984). In the US, overtime levels rose during and after the Second World War, but stabilized during the late 1960s and 70s at around three-and-a-half hours average per manual worker (Hedges and Taylor 1980).

In both Britain and other countries maintaining high levels of overtime, the amount of overtime worked has been remarkably resistant to economic conditions, remaining high even during periods of recession and spare labour capacity. Partly this reflects management's reliance on overtime to counter short-term, extraordinary circumstances. However, a significant proportion of total overtime worked is systematic in nature — that is worked on a regular basis and incorporated into the weekly work schedule rather than as an element of worktime to be drawn upon only in emergencies. The decision to utilize overtime can be a complex one, with management weighing the extra costs of premium-paid worktime (average overtime premia for manual men in Britain is a little under time and a half) against a number of factors such as the flexibility gained and the avoidance of costs of hiring additional labour. The growing level of non-wage labour costs in recent years (costs of holidays, pension and sickness schemes, redundancies, etc.) has tended to increase the cost of hiring additional manpower and thus has acted in favour of utilizing overtime rather than recruiting extra labour to meet production requirements (Hart 1984).

Table 3 Changes in overtime working among manual workers in British manufacturing industries

	% of all operatives working overtime	Average overtime hours per operative	Actual hours (million)
1965	34.6	9.0	17.83
1970	34.4	8.9	17.33
1975	30.3	8.3	13.55
1977	34.6	8.7	15.58
1979	34.2	8.7	15.07
1980	29.5	8.3	11.76
1981	26.6	8.2	9.37
1982	29.8	8.3	9.93
1983	31.5	8.5	10.19
1984	34.3	8.9	11.39
1985	34.0	9.0	11.98
1986	34.2	9.0	11.72
1987	36.1	9.3	12.68
1988 (April)	37.6	9.1	13.03

Source: *Employment Gazette*, No. 1, February 1987; *Employment Gazette*, October 1987; and *Employment Gazette*, June 1988.

For trade unions, overtime poses a dilemma which remains unresolved. In Britain, for example, the TUC and individual unions have expressed their opposition to overtime, arguing that it increases unemployment during times of recession, impinges on workers' leisure time, and also allows employers to maintain low basic rates since final earnings are made tolerable by overtime payments. Some analysis of overtime indeed points to a tendency for overtime to be prevalent in certain industries typified by lower-than-average rates of pay and among workers on low basic pay rates (Trade Union Research Unit 1981; NBPI 1970). However, the relationship between rates of pay and overtime is not clear-cut; some industries with low basic pay do not maintain high rates of overtime and likewise some high paying industries also exhibit above average overtime (Kinchin-Smith and Palmer 1981).

115

On the other hand, however, local union organizations have tended to be far less critical of overtime working, responding instead to the widespread willingness among employees to work overtime in order to boost earnings. In a 1970 study of over 2,000 establishments, the National Board for Prices and Incomes found that in more than half the cases, local union organizations accepted or even encouraged overtime, while in almost all of the remainder, the unions were neutral on this issue; in less than half of one per cent of cases were local unions opposed to the practice of overtime working (NBPI 1970). Moreover, once this trading-off of leisure for income has begun, expectations and spending patterns will tend to adjust upwards, increasing further workers' desire to work overtime (Whybrew, 1968). This seems to be particularly true for those groups whose financial commitments are highest, such as married men in their 30s and 40s (see, for example, Kats and Goldberg 1982).

Periodically, overtime has shifted nearer to the industrial relations centre stage as management has sought its elimination or a more effective use of overtime working. For example a reduction in overtime represented a key management objective in many productivity agreements in the 1960s and 70s. In the Fawley agreements, for example, one of the key changes in working practices sought by management was a reduction in overtime levels from their level of as much as 18 per cent of total hours to 2 per cent (Flanders 1964). Likewise, more than a decade later in the productivity agreements reached in the Post Office, the reduction of overtime (and particularly the elimination of the very high rates of overtime worked by the London 'overtime kings') was a central management objective in the changed working practices (Upton 1982; Osborn and Blyton 1985). Typically, productivity negotiations sought agreement on reducing overtime by consolidating at least part of previous overtime earnings into basic pay. Overtime has also been an issue in recent flexibility negotiations (examined in more detail below). In partial contrast to earlier periods, however, the current emphasis tends to be either on the use of overtime to cover unusually busy periods (rather than to meet regular workload) or the introduction of more flexible rostering such that work beyond what was formally defined as normal hours is treated not as overtime but as part of an (expandable) normal day compensated by fewer work hours on a later day rather than by additional payment.

Shiftwork

Overtime and shiftwork represent the principal means of extending the period of daily productive activity. Shiftwork may be introduced for various reasons — for example for technical requirements in continuous process industries, for essential safety and maintenance work or to maintain the availability of a public service such as hospital and transport services. Increasingly significant too is the development of shiftworking to maximize equipment utilization. As capital intensity grows, so does the incentive to reap maximum benefit from the investment to repay the capital outlay and minimize the cost of rapid obsolescence.

In the postwar period, shiftwork has steadily increased in industrialized countries — the ILO estimates that the number of workers engaged in shiftwork doubled between 1950 and 1974 (ILO 1978). Nevertheless, despite this general increase, different countries display marked variations in the proportion of the labour force which works shifts.

Table 4 Shiftworking in nine European countries, late 1970s (service sector not included)

Country	% involved in shiftwork	Sectors with most shift work
Belgium	26.6	Cars, energy, minerals
Denmark	14	Paper, chemicals
West Germany	20	Energy, chemicals, metals
France	31.3	Metals, paper, textiles
Ireland	18.8	Textiles, chemicals, paper
Italy	22	Metals, paper, non-metallic minerals
Luxembourg	41.5	Metals, chemicals, fibres
Netherlands	10.6	Food products, textiles, metals
United Kingdom	30	Cars, metals, chemicals

Source: European Trade Union Institute (1979) *Reductions of Working Time in Western Europe, Part 1*, Brussels: ETUI, p. 59.

From Table 4 it is evident that in the late 1970s, Denmark and the Netherlands maintained relatively low levels of shiftworking, while France, Luxembourg and the UK exhibited much higher levels. In Britain in recent years shiftworking has increased steadily except in the 1980–3 recessionary period. Bosworth and Dawkins (1980) note that between 1954 and 1978, the proportion of manual workers engaged in shiftworking increased from one in eight workers to one

117

in three. Outside Europe, shiftwork levels also vary, with for example the United States operating a comparatively high level of shiftworking (Finn 1981; Lehmann 1980), while Japan has traditionally maintained a somewhat lower level — around one in eight workers in the mid 70s according to the ILO, though significantly higher in the manufacturing sector (Fudge 1980).

Yet though involving as many as one in three manual workers in Britain and elsewhere, and despite being associated with considerable psychological and social disruptions, shiftwork *per se* has rarely represented a major theme on trade union or industrial relations agenda. 'Most unions,' comment Evans and Palmer 'have come to accept the inevitability of shiftworking and to concentrate their efforts on ensuring the best possible pay and other employment conditions for their members' (1985: 152). There have, however, been some notable exceptions to this general lack of conflict over the development of shiftwork practices. One case is the flexible rostering dispute on the British railways in 1982, which involved the unions initially rejecting a plan to make shift lengths more flexible, so as to improve the scheduling of railway drivers' timetables and increase the productive time-use above the previous average of 3 hrs 20 minutes for an eight-hour shift (Starkey 1986). As we discuss further in the final section, this move by the railway management is now being repeated elsewhere as one means by which managements are seeking to reduce unit labour costs and increase manpower flexibility.

Aside from the flexible rostering dispute, the other main shiftworking issue to arouse significant union interest and comment has been the consideration of new shiftwork systems, particularly the move from four- to five-crew working. Currently most continuous shiftwork systems utilize a four-crew system, with three shift crews working on any one day and the fourth enjoying a rest day. However, as the length of the basic work week falls below forty hours, this four-crew system involves a considerable element of in-built overtime, each of the four crews working forty-two hours per week (one quarter of the 168 total weekly hours). To reflect the changes in working hours and reduce the level of overtime working, increasing numbers of companies in several countries have commenced five- (or even six-) crew working. With its link with reduced working hours and possible additional employment, various trade unions and union federations (including the GMB in Britain, the CFDT in France and the United Federation of Italian Unions) have expressed support for this shiftwork arrangement (Blyton 1985). An earlier Dutch study also found a greater willingness among workers to accept shiftworking under a five-crew arrangement compared to the four crew system (Voogd 1978).

As shiftworking continues to increase and spreads into occupations and grades with no previous tradition of shiftwork arrangements — for example white-collar occupations in certain technical and computer-related fields (see Blandy 1984) — the unions representing these grades may take a fresh interest in shiftwork patterns and the means by which any health and social effects can be offset. Such an interest is an extension of existing trade union involvement in health and safety issues. Central in the shiftwork and health issue is the question of night working, with night shifts identified as far more disruptive of physiological rhythms than other shifts. There is some indication that the extent of night-working is declining; however, in Britain, the 1986 Sex Discrimination Act reduced the restrictions on women's nightwork in industrial undertakings from February 1988, which may lead to some reversal of this decline particularly during a period of economic revival.

Holidays

The growth in paid holiday entitlement has been marked in recent years particularly in Western European countries. In the early 1960s, the norm in many industrial countries was two weeks' paid vacation (excluding public holidays). By the mid-1980s, this had more than doubled; four weeks' annual paid holiday is now a general minimum within Western Europe, and several countries (e.g. Austria, Denmark, Finland, France, Luxembourg, Spain and Sweden) now operate a legal minimum of five weeks' paid holiday (EIRR 1987). In some countries bargained agreements have extended this further; in West Germany, for example, almost two-thirds (65 per cent) of employees were entitled to six weeks' annual holiday by the end of 1986 (IDS 1987).

This general trend is reflected in Britain. The length of basic entitlement increased only slowly until the late 1960s, when the average manual worker entitlement stood at two-and-a-half weeks. During the 1970s paid holidays increased considerably and continued to do so in the 1980s; by the end of 1985, average basic holiday entitlement was almost 4½ weeks (22 working days) and a third of manual workers received additional service-related holidays. Despite this increase in manual workers' holidays, average holiday entitlement of non-manual workers in Britain remains higher than their manual counterparts, though by the 1980s the differential had

119

significantly reduced compared to a decade earlier (*Employment Gazette*, December 1981).

The holiday pattern in the United States and Japan contrasts markedly with this European pattern. By the end of the 1970s, average paid holidays in the United States had increased little beyond two weeks, a level little changed from the 1960s (Hedges and Taylor 1980). A small percentage (about 5 per cent) of collective bargaining agreements do include provision for extended vacations of around three months for long serving workers, as in the steel industry. However, as with weekly hours, it seems that holiday entitlement has not been as prominent an issue in the US as it has in Western Europe. Possibly, the early achievement of a relatively short working week shifted union attention in the US more markedly away from greater leisure to maximizing income.

In Japan too, paid holidays have lagged behind the European increases and current average holiday entitlement is around fifteen days (Shimada and Hayami 1986: 215). This differential between European and Japanese holiday entitlement is heightened by the common practice of Japanese employees working part of their holiday allocation to increase income. On average Japanese workers take only 8.7 days (58 per cent) of their holiday entitlement (ibid: 215). Further, despite the growing profile of parties of Japanese tourists gazing at the sights in the capitals of Western Europe, for most Japanese workers the tendency is to take only very short holidays of one or two days (Hanami 1980).

In countries where holiday entitlement has increased substantially, one important explanation for this is that in many situations increasing holidays can represent a lower cost option for reducing working time than cutting the length of the working week. Further, by restricting some of the recent holiday increase to shut-down periods (as has happened widely in Britain in relation to the Christmas–New Year period) this provides a period for plant maintenance, ensures a predictable effect of the time reduction on production, and avoids the need for cover compared to where holidays are left to individual discretion. Faced with trade union demands for reduced working time (particularly demands for a thirty-five hour working week) employers have shown themselves more disposed to counter this demand with an offer to increase holiday provision. Five days' increase in holiday entitlement is approximately equivalent to a one-hour reduction in the working week. Employees too (particularly male employees) have shown themselves to be generally more in favour of increased holidays than small reductions in the working week, with additional full days holiday being seen as providing more useful non-work time than minor changes to the working day (Best 1980).

Despite this value attached to increased holidays, the rise in entitlement which has taken place has gone only part way to extending individual discretion over the annual pattern of working time. In the 1970s, a number of commentators on working time argued the benefits of a greater availability of longer periods away from work in the form of extended vacations or sabbatical leave (Dickson 1975; Jenkins and Sherman 1979). As we have noted, some American unions have gone some way in negotiating extended leave arrangements — thereby partly offsetting the relatively low level of average paid vacations in the US. In addition, the growing interest in 'annual hours' contracts, whereby working time is calculated on an annual rather than a weekly basis, can in some instances offer scope for a more flexible approach to holiday provision (Lynch 1985). At the same time, for shift workers (and in Britain these contracts are mainly confined to shift workers in continuous process industries), annual hours agreements act to blur the distinction between holidays and rest days, and indeed between weekdays and weekends (Desmons and Vidal-Hall 1987). Overall, however, for the majority of working populations, the recent increase in holiday entitlement has not been accompanied by significantly greater discretion, such as in the ability to 'carry over' unused holiday to form much longer periods of leave every few years.

After a period of considerable expansion in holiday provision, trade union attention has tended to shift in the last years from the question of holidays back to the perennial issue of the length of the working week. In the FRG, for example, the period of expansion in holidays (and earlier retirement; see below) was followed in the early 80s by renewed union efforts in engineering and other industries to secure a thirty-five hour week. In Britain, attention has begun to shift back not only to the working week — at the time of writing, postal and engineering workers are pursuing a claim for a shorter working week — but also to the organization of working-time; the management pursuit of greater flexibility in worktime arrangements is considered in a later section of this chapter.

Short-Time Working

While overtime is used to extend the length of the working day, short-time working produces the opposite effect, reducing the hours of some or all of a workforce. Short-time working is essentially a short-term response to maintain the level of employment during an economic downturn. If the downturn is considered to be temporary, short-time working has a number of potential benefits for employers compared to redundancies, including the retention of skilled workers, and the avoidance of redundancy payments and later recruiting and training costs (Reid 1982). Short-time working is also generally preferable to redundancy both for the individuals concerned and for national governments concerned to minimize any increase in unemployment — so much so, in fact, that at different times several countries have devised compensated short-time working schemes to encourage its use in favour of the redundancy option. In Europe, the Federal Republic of Germany has been particularly active in this area; state subsidy of short-time working in Germany dates back more than half a century. The current provisions stem from a 1969 Act which, if certain conditions are met (relating to numbers involved and period of short-time working), provides an allowance equal to 68 per cent of lost earnings. The length of time this is paid varies with the situation in the industry affected, and the level of unemployment in a region; in the case of the iron and steel industry for example, the normal maximum period of six months payment was extended to three years in the early 1980s recession (Meisel 1984; Blyton 1985: 93–4). A similar, though more restricted scheme was introduced in Britain in 1979, the Temporary Short-Time Working Compensation Scheme (TSTWCS). Initially this provided for an allowance of 75 per cent of normal pay for up to twelve months; however, this was progressively reduced and by 1982 had been cut to 50 per cent for up to six months.

The level of short-time working tends to be high in the early stages of recession, when there is uncertainty as to the severity of the downturn and the necessity for redundancies. As the recession continues, however, support for short-term measures declines; moreover as redundancies are made, the viability of further short-time working among those remaining is reduced. Hence in Britain in the post 1979 recession, the peak of short-time working was reached in March 1981 when 984,000 workers were on short-time. By 1983, however, this had reduced to an average of just 79,000 and further declined to 28,000 by 1985.

In this area of short-time working, North America has lagged behind Europe. Generally, the unemployment benefit regulations have militated against short-time working by restricting benefit to employees workless for whole weeks. However, increased interest in compensated short-time working schemes in the late 1970s and early 1980s led to some easing of the Unemployment Insurance (UI) conditions in Canada and several US states (notably California) to provide compensation for workers laid-off for part of the week (Blyton 1985: 95–7). These amendments to UI legislation were generally introduced on a temporary, experimental basis. However, initial reactions in Canada in 1979 led to the re-introduction of short-time working compensation in 1982 (Reid and Meltz 1984). Similar positive reactions in California and elsewhere would suggest that short-time working is likely to become a more prominent working-time response in future periods of economic downturn in North America.

One reason which may have held back the development of short-time working in North America is the ambivalent response by the trade unions to short-time working. Bednaznik (1980) has indicated that provision for reduced hours actually became *less* common in bargaining agreements between the 1950s and the mid 1970s. Primarily this reflects the strong seniority principles in American unionism and the tendency for senior employees to prefer the laying-off of workers with less length of service, to the more widespread impact of hours reductions. Also in Canada, national union organizations have tended to be critical of short-time working schemes, which are seen to divert attention from the main issue of restoring full employment (Reid 1982). In contrast, trade unions in Europe, where the seniority principle is far less marked, have been much more supportive of compensated short-time working schemes, particularly in those industries most hit by recession (TUC 1981; Blyton 1985: 99).

Retirement

While much of the attention on working-time has been directed to the length of the working week, and to a lesser extent the working year, significant changes have also occurred in recent years to the length of the working lifetime. In part this reflects changes in the age of entry to the labour force, resulting from a raising of the school leaving age (it is now sixteen years in France, Norway, Spain, Sweden and the UK, and eighteen years in Belgium) and more recently the introduction of government-sponsored training and other schemes to improve the transition from school to work and react to the high level of youth unemployment in the early 1980s. The growth in adult unemployment has also led to a reduction in aggregate working time. However, for those maintaining their employed status, the total span of working-time has been affected by changes taking place in the average age of retirement.

Having long been a side issue for trade unions and personnel managers, the retirement question has become more prominent as a result of the spread of occupational pension schemes and the increased use of early retirement to reduce manpower levels. In Britain, approximately half of the workforce (and a much higher proportion in the public sector) were members of an occupational pension scheme at the beginning of the 1980s (White 1980). With retirement provision representing an important (albeit deferred) element of remuneration, trade unions have become increasingly involved in pension negotiations. However, the complexity of pension fund management is one of several factors which has generally resulted in very little employee influence to date on the way occupational pensions are managed or distributed (Schuller 1986).

In terms of establishing favourable early retirement provisions, however, trade unions have been rather more successful. Faced with an oversupply of labour, early retirement has become widely regarded by both management and unions as a more acceptable vehicle for reducing manpower than compulsory redundancy (though not infrequently the former approach is a euphemism for the latter). Early retirement schemes would seem to be particularly used either as one element in a broader labour-shedding activity, where the pressures for manpower reduction are not immediate, or at the beginning of a manpower reduction programme. In the early stages of the post-1979 recession in Britain, for example, White (1980) found that almost one-third of manufacturing companies had utilized early retirement to reduce the size of their payroll; the proportion rose to more than half in those companies which were also reducing manpower by other means.

In the later 1970s, early retirement schemes were introduced in many industrial countries, and operated on a national, sector, or individual company basis. National early retirement schemes currently operate in such countries as Austria, Belgium, Denmark, West Germany, Greece, Norway and Spain. Examples of sector schemes include workers in the Austrian and Luxembourg iron and steel industries, mining in France and the UK, fishing in Portugal, and railways in France. Together with the higher level of unemployment among older age groups, these various schemes have lowered the participation rate of older workers in the labour market considerably. For example, by 1980 only a third of German males between sixty and sixty-five were employed (Standing 1986: 330). By the mid-1980s, the average age of retirement for manual workers in West Germany was just under fifty-eight years, and 60.5 years for non-manuals (Bosch 1986b: 273).

124

More recently, rather less prominence has been given to early retirement, partly due to reduced pressure to cut manpower levels and partly because some of the earlier schemes have proved costly to maintain. One effect of the latter has been a somewhat greater examination of lower cost alternatives such as partial or 'phased' retirement. In Britain, both the TUC and CBI have expressed support for phased retirement through progressive reductions in working-time. However in practice, such schemes remain rare; only in Sweden has a partial retirement scheme been operating on a nationwide basis for some years, though similar schemes were introduced in 1987 in Denmark and Finland (Blyton 1984, 1989a).

THE SEARCH FOR GREATER WORK-TIME FLEXIBILITY

While the question of reducing working-time continues to feature on many industrial relations agendas, the issue of duration is increasingly being linked to, or even upstaged by, the call for greater working-time flexibility. 'In the recent bargaining rounds of nations so different as the Federal Republic of Germany, the Netherlands, the Scandinavian and the Mediterranean countries', concluded Treu (1986: 9) recently, 'flexibility has been the major *quid pro quo* required and obtained by employers for working-time reduction.'

Clearly, the search for greater flexibility extends beyond working-time issues to more general questions of organizational structure, including the ability to respond rapidly to market changes. One effect of the growing influence of Japanese management styles has been to give added prominence to functional flexibility (e.g. multi-skilled workers and the lack of craft demarcations) and labour market flexibility (e.g. the mix of permanent and temporary workers). Working-time arrangements represent an additional potential source of manpower flexibility, particularly in regard to re-designing work schedules to maximize the productive use of worktime and respond to changing operational demands, technological developments and turbulent markets.

Of course, there is nothing new in identifying working-time as a flexible resource. Following our earlier discussion, overtime and short-time working are longstanding examples of how basic working-time arrangements can be amended to match a change in circumstances. The long-term growth in shiftworking and the development of new shiftwork arrangements and annual hours contracts represent other responses to extending the productive period. The growth

125

in the demand for part-time jobs can also be explained partly by a desire to use labour time at periods of greatest need. This is particularly evident in the retail industry, where part-time working has grown considerably, partly to meet the lunchtime peak in shopping activity. More generally, the large-scale growth in the service sector has led to a considerable flexibilization of worktime arrangements, particularly in those services which operate either outside normal working hours (e.g. transport, restaurants, hotels) or continuously (hospitals and other emergency services).

In the 1970s, much attention was given to time flexibility as a means of increasing employee choice over start and stop times (and also incidentally reducing a number of managerial problems such as the supervision of those times). By 1980, approximately one in twelve workers in Britain were covered by some form of flexitime arrangement. The flexitime systems introduced then have generally continued and even expanded in terms of the flexibility allowed and the range of occupations covered (though this arrangement is still concentrated in the white-collar sector). A recent example of expansion is in Britain's Inland Revenue, where previous restrictions have been relaxed to allow employees to build up more credit hours and thereby take up to two weeks' extra leave in additional days off work (*Financial Times*, 26/1/87). However, while these flexitime systems have been maintained and even extended, the emphasis in recent years has shifted to other forms of time flexibility. The growth in international competition and increased capital investment, together with the desire to reduce costs and minimize the effects of reductions in total working-time, have been among a series of factors encouraging employers to seek a more productive use of working-time, by breaking established notions of the working day and week and re-scheduling worktime to gain more profitable use from plant and equipment. In this endeavour, the current priority given to time flexibility reflects more accurately the 1960s' concern with productivity agreements than the 1970s' employee-centred interest in flexitime. As noted above, a key feature of many of the early productivity agreements was the management objective of re-establishing control over working time by reducing the extent of, and reliance upon, a high degree of overtime working.

A number of major negotiations and disputes both in Britain and abroad in the 1980s have also reflected this heightened attention to working-time patterns and the productive use (and definition) of the 'normal' working day. In Britain, the most prominent dispute in this category is the 'flexible rostering' dispute in 1982 involving the members of the Associated Society of Locomotive Engineers and Firemen (ASLEF) and the British Railways Board. Central to the dispute (which also involved a pay rise and a reduction of the working week to thirty-nine hours) was the introduction of flexible rostering, which abandoned the fixed eight-hour day and allowed for rosters varying between seven and nine hours, to allow a more effective matching of worktime and operational requirements. ASLEF's complaints were that the ending of the standard day (in existence since 1919) would add to the strain of their members' jobs, and also result in a loss of jobs. A reluctance to compromise (which Ferner (1985) argues was partly due to management's desire to demonstrate to the government its commitment to productivity increases) led to a two-week strike in 1982, in which the union was defeated and required to accept flexible rostering.

A similar issue arose in another two-week strike in early 1987 involving 110,000 British Telecom engineers. Having established a shorter working week in the 1970s (which had effectively established a nine-day fortnight for telecom engineers by 1978 — a work pattern more common in Australia than in Britain; see Symons 1978) the pay settlement and efficiency measures sought by Telecom management involved significant changes to the working day. Among these efficiency measures (or 'job re-patterning packages' as they were rather ponderously titled) was the proposal to change shift-patterns and move to a longer working day, thereby scheduling more time into the most profitable afternoon period. In the event the more radical of the proposed shift changes were finally dropped by management, though the definition of the normal working day was extended by three-quarters of an hour.

Two other industries which have recently demonstrated a greater management search for time flexibility have been coal and engineering. British Coal have proposed new working-time arrangements for thirteen existing and proposed collieries. In two, located in the North East, this entails longer shifts to offset the greater travelling time to distant coal faces. Most attention, however, has been focused on the proposed six-day working at a new pit in Margam, South Wales, and in several other collieries in England and Scotland. The development of Margam is said by management to be dependent on agreement on six-day working. While at the time of writing there appears a willingness among the South Wales National Union of Mineworkers to accept the new working arrangements (and thereby secure the 800 jobs which have been announced for the Margam operation), the national union leadership currently opposes flexibility, partly on grounds that it would result in substantial job losses due to higher productivity and would also break a forty-year agreement guaranteeing five-day working. Though detailed working schedules have not been announced, one proposal to cover the six-day 'coaling' is for miners to be rostered for three weeks of six morning, afternoon and night shifts followed by one week off.

In the British engineering industry, negotiations over a shorter working week began again in 1983, following the one-hour reduction to 39 hours in 1981. Since that time the greater application of computer-based and other technologies, together with the developments in flexibility relating to skill-boundaries and other demarcations, have further stimulated management's search for more productive time arrangements. The 1987 negotiations over hours (at least temporarily broken off by the unions at the time of writing) involve a management offer of two-stage phased reduction from thirty-nine to 37½ hours by May 1989 in return for greater job flexibility, including changes in working-time schedules. Specifically, the working-time changes would give management greater freedom to accommodate fluctuations in the flow of work by varying basic weekly hours during the year (providing the 37½ hour average was achieved over the year as a whole). There is evidence that similar developments are also taking place in other parts of Europe. For example, just as the British and West German engineering industries experienced major disputes over the working week issue in the late 1970s and early 1980s, so too the current linking of duration and flexibility in the British engineering industry follows a pattern established in its West German counterpart after the 1984 dispute. As Bosch (1986b) reports, the 38.5 hour settlement in West Germany was conditional on local flexibility agreements on the implementation of the reduction. For example, while the overall reduction of company work hours was to be 38.5, the time of individual work groups could conceivably vary from thirty-seven to forty hours depending on 'the needs of the enterprise'. The settlement also allowed the weekly hours to be distributed evenly or unevenly across five working days. In the event individual differentiation of working-time around the 38.5 hour average was agreed in only a very small number of enterprises. However, inter-group variation was much more evident in the implementation of the 1½ hours reduction (via shorter days, free days, longer meal breaks, shorter weeks, etc; see Bosch 1986b: 284). Subsequent agreements, which take basic hours in the West German metal-working industry down to thirty-seven by 1989, have further extended management's scope to introduce greater flexibility over the scheduling of work hours (Incomes Data Services 1987).

Other analyses of the European labour market have similarly highlighted the increased and continuing emphasis on labour flexibility including the area of work-time flexibility (e.g. Standing 1986). So great is the emphasis in fact that Bosch (1986a: 161) comments that in all developed capitalist countries, flexibility is being exalted as a 'magic charm', capable of delivering benefits to all in ways that previous employment policies have failed to do.

CONCLUSIONS

From the beginnings of trade unionism, the temporal boundaries of the wage-effort bargain have been a persistent focus of attention. The growth in the power of organized labour, together with steady increases in labour productivity have been translated into a marked reduction in total working-time over the last century: average annual working-time is now only half that worked in the textile mills during the first decades of the nineteenth century. Reductions in working-time have occurred in steps rather than as a continuous decline. Following a cut in working-time, the desire for further reductions (rather than, for example, increased income) temporarily recedes. Partly, this reflects a shift in perceptions of the marginal utility of more leisure compared to higher income (see chapter 4). In addition, however, other longer-term factors are also relevant in anticipating the strength of future demands for reduced worktime. For example, in the nineteenth and early twentieth centuries, an important element in the reduced-hours campaign was the hard physical toil inherent in many manual jobs. In more recent times, the physical demands of many manual jobs has tended to decline (though certainly not disappear), with the growing scale of production and the application of more mechanization to production and the movement of materials (coal-mining is a good example of this, particularly in mines with seam widths sufficient to allow a high degree of mechanized working).

At the same time, not only are a number of unions currently pursuing further reductions in working hours, but also the working-time issue has been given fresh impetus from managements seeking more efficient organization of working-time. The recent prominence given to achieving greater worktime flexibility is part of a broader search for more flexible approaches to organization and production. Growing competition has provoked this search; technological change has facilitated it. The versatility of contemporary manufacturing equipment enables management to maximize economies of scope rather than simply economies of scale.

At many points, the development of greater enterprise flexibility impacts upon personnel and industrial relations policies and practice. Here we have been considering recent working-time changes, though for trade unions this management search for flexibility also incorporates issues relating to work function (e.g. skill definitions and extent of demarcation), contract (temporary *vs.* permanent workers, in-house *vs.* contracted-out labour), and regulation (concerning wage levels, bargaining arrangements, and protective legislation). With other changes occurring in work patterns — notably the growth in part-time working — these developments represent a progressive undermining of the traditional workforce of full-time, permanent workers — the group in which trade unionism has in the past, been strongest. We have highlighted a number of instances where unions have resisted (or at least sought to exact a significant price for) working-time innovations. Generally these innovations have involved changing previous working-time arrangements to increase the efficiency of labour-time. Yet unlike in the 1970s, when the interests of management and workers were seen to coincide in the development of 'flexitime' systems, in the late 1980s, potential conflicts of interest over flexibility are more evident, reflecting the managerial orientation of recent innovations to extend worktime flexibility, and the challenge to hard-won agreements that these represent, such as over length of working day and the weekend break from work.

This search for greater flexibility in labour use shows no signs of abating; indeed it is likely to increase as competition intensifies and further capital intensification heightens the importance of securing maximum utilization of plant and equipment. Future working-time reductions can be expected to be linked, more closely than in the past, with changes in the scheduling of working-time. For the trade union movement, the pattern of working-time (shiftwork systems, overtime, the definitions of the working day, working week and so on) looks set to become as prominent an issue in the late twentieth century as issues of worktime duration were in the late nineteenth century. Bosch (1986a: 161) argues that in the future pursuit of greater work-time flexibility, there must undoubtedly be areas in which employers' and workers' interests overlap. However, with the power of unions relatively weakened in those countries where high unemployment persists, it is problematic to what extent labour's representatives will be able to ensure how far the flexibility changes will reflect these areas of mutual interest.

NOTES

1. Generalizations across the US are complicated, however, by the variations in different industries and regions. Edwards (1979: 62), for example, cites a study of hours in iron and steel in 1919 where the average of sixty-six hours per week was more than 20 per cent higher than the average for other industries. Similarly, Evans (1969) notes that in the 1920s, hours were considerably longer in the non-union Southern States than in the more unionized North.

2. The Netherlands is a notable late exception to this general tendency. The forty-five hour week was achieved nationally in the Netherlands only in 1962; a forty-hour week was generally achieved by 1975 (Visser 1986: 225).

7

Conclusions

The starting point in the preceding chapters has been the centrality of time in organizational life; a centrality reflected in management preoccupations and worker experience. Yet the very ubiquity of the temporal dimension in organization and experience has worked against its detailed study by more than a handful of researchers spread thinly across time and academic disciplines. Amongst others who have noted the significance of time as they hurry *en route* to some other research destination, the tendency has been to treat time as a homogeneous entity: linear, unambiguous, and non-problematic. If the foregoing essays have shown anything, it is firstly that more focused research on the temporal factor would be well rewarded in terms of greater insight into organizational processes and worker experience; and secondly that those embarking on such a journey would be better equipped if they set off with a conception of time which anticipated a heterogeneity in time-reckoning and time-experience among organizational members.

It is not our intention in this conclusion to summarize the many and diverse issues considered in earlier parts. Rather we wish to draw attention to some key themes which have emerged, themes which would repay more extensive (and intensive) investigation. At a number of points, for example, emphasis has been laid on the contrast between a quantitative approach to time, and its relevance to measuring, controlling and rewarding individual performance; and a more qualitative approach to the study of time, which provides more opportunity to identify and explain the variations in the experience of worktime and the informal time-reckoning systems which modify formal time patterns as defined by management, individual work contracts, and collective agreements. In a busy and growth-orientated industrial society, it is time-scarcity which dominates management (and often union) thinking, with the finite nature of time encouraging concentration on how best to use this scarce resource through more efficient co-ordination of activities, increased pace of operations and/or the extension of the productive work period. The precedence of the objective aspects of worktime has been at the expense of greater subjective assessment of the experience of worktime, and its informal organization. In practice, however, subjective and objective considerations are inseparable, with an understanding of each being essential to the full appreciation of how time systems operate in work organizations, and how objective temporal conditions are modified by subjective experience. As Starkey pointed out in Chapter 3, the way individuals experience time is not only a complex issue, but is also a central factor in determining why some people suffer undue stress in their jobs, and why others find it so difficult to adapt to unemployment and its weakening of time structures. Other issues, including the degrees of job satisfaction and alienation, the relationship between work and non-work experience and attitudes towards retirement each have a close affiliation to the individual's experience of worktime. In turn, the variety, pacing, and sequencing of tasks play important roles in the formation and perception of that experience.

INTENSIFICATION OF TIME

Temporal aspects of organization, including the control of time-related costs and the efficiency of working-time arrangements at the individual or group level, are implicit or explicit in many of the managerial concerns and techniques in vogue in the late 1980s. Foremost amongst these, at least in manufacturing, are the 'just-in-time' systems of production scheduling and inventory control. By reducing (or even eliminating) stocks of raw materials, components and finished goods, JIT seeks to minimize any periods of unproductive time in which expensive capital is tied up. Such a system not only requires dependable suppliers and efficient communications from the market place, but also imposes considerable reliance on the effectiveness of internal organizational co-ordination and the timing of the production process. One North American auto plant, for example, has car seats delivered *every twenty minutes*, with the managerial objective of ensuring that no seat remains in stock for more than forty minutes. Clearly such a system can operate only if the communication between production controllers and suppliers (not to mention the transportation system) is highly efficient and reliable. Whilst minimizing the cost of holding

133

stocks, such a highly developed JIT system puts considerable pressure on the timing of operations in general, and the split-minute (perhaps soon the split-second) arrival of components at the appropriate work station in particular.

In important part the accelerated pursuit of minimum stock levels, and production-to-order rather than stock, stem from other developments which have a time-related dimension, and in particular the application of computer-based technologies. Advances in information technology and telecommunications have enabled the transfer of information to become virtually instantaneous, irrespective of the distance between the parties involved. It has even been argued that systems may become too efficient; the 1987 stock market crash for example has been attributed by some to the efficiency of communications between markets and the absence of time-lags which could have engendered more measured responses. Overall, however, the growth of computer technology, and advances in electronic mail and other communications systems, have been used as the basis for reducing time uncertainty, and increasing the efficiency of organizational time. Other technological advances — for example in design and assembly functions — have had similar time implications, allowing for much faster production and adjustment of design specifications, and a more intensive pace of production. The refinement of word-processors has had a similar effect on the office, with various operations (for example re-drafting and multiple circulation) being carried out many times faster than with traditional typewriter systems.

TEMPORAL FLEXIBILITY

In addition to being one of the motors driving the search for increased time-efficiency, improved scheduling of production and more effective warehouse management, current technology (and especially the capacity for more flexible operations which that technology brings) has formed part of the impetus behind the drive for increased manpower flexibility. The dimensions of manpower flexibility are interdependent, with functional flexibility being a natural concommitant to temporal flexibility, so that increased manpower flexibility brings with it increased management control over task, duration, and scheduling of activities, usually rationalized by the pursuit of minimum costs. This 'Holy Grail' has dominated management thinking in recent years, leading to the demand for greater productivity and greater efficiency in response to markets perceived as more competitive, more international, and, in the case of traditional industries such as coal, steel and shipbuilding, greatly reduced. As we noted in Chapter 6, the social organization of production, and in particular the organization of labour time, already figures prominently in these efforts to increase efficiency. There are no signs that this effort is about to diminish; on the contrary, increased interest in new shiftwork patterns, together with variable, annual and flexible hours arrangements indicate that the scheduling of worktime is becoming as prominent an issue on the managerial agenda as its overall duration.

Among business economists this revival of interest in working-time has re-kindled interest in the relationship between hours of work, costs, and performance. Among the questions addressed in Chapter 4 is the relationship between hours and employment: on the one hand the relative costs of achieving extra output via additional hours or additional employment, and on the other the extent to which cuts in hours may provide a basis for additional employment opportunities. Trade unions have periodically championed this latter argument, advocating worktime reductions as a response to unemployment. This issue has been addressed elsewhere by both Blyton and Hill, amongst others (Blyton and Hill 1981; Blyton 1985, 1987; Hill 1984, 1987). At present, however, the central time-related question facing trade unions is not the relationship between hours and employment, but that of formulating an appropriate response to managerial demands for greater worktime flexibility. As we have seen, such issues are prominent in primary (particularly coal), secondary (e.g. engineering) and tertiary (e.g. post and telecommunications) sectors. To date the scope for union response to this (and other) forms of flexibility has been subject only to limited investigation (although see Fairbrother 1987). What is needed also is a much clearer picture of the various forms which manpower flexibility is taking in particular contexts and how these are related to different technological and other changes. Up to now, much of the literature on flexibility, including working time-changes, has given the impression of a uniform growth of various flexible arrangements. Yet at the level of the individual firm, this uniformity may be more apparent than real, with different combinations of technical, organizational and market (including labour market) circumstances giving rise to a host of varying developments in the utilization of labour.

MANAGEMENT OF TIME

The temporal dimension is not only evident in the current managerial

135

interest in JIT and manpower flexibility; it also figures prominently at the level of individual managerial performance. This is most evident in the growth of 'time management' programmes. These involve the detailed logging of how time is allocated at work (a process which often reveals the inability of managers to delegate responsibilities effectively), followed by a re-appraisal of time-consuming activities and the ultimate adoption of a more time-conscious (and time-decisive) approach to the various tasks which comprise the typical management role. Behind such techniques lie the familiar notions of time scarcity, the costs associated with time and the potential performance gains from the effective management of time. This self-administered 'time and motion' study, whilst an increasingly popular part of management development programmes, appears however to be doing little to reduce the average hours worked by many individual managers —one large study of British managers in the early 1980s found that over 40 per cent worked on average more than fifty hours per week (Poole *et al.* 1981).

While the time of individual managers may be receiving more detailed study, other aspects of individual working-time are conspicuously absent from research agendas. In the economic analysis of working-time in Chapter 4, Hill pointed to the importance of individual preferences in the worktime decision, whilst recognizing the institutional constraints on the full exercise of those preferences. Despite its importance, little direct research has been conducted on preferences, and what has been done has tended to be either at a fairly general level (such as investigating whether those working part-time are doing so as a first choice or as a response to the absence of full-time job opportunities), or via the overly hypothetical approach of surveying individual preferences towards some future combinations of higher earnings and lower hours (see for example Best 1980). If, as we anticipate, working-time is to shift further away from uniform and rigid patterns towards more diverse schedules, with a variety of working-time patterns operating within and across organizations, then the scope for matching individual and organizational time preferences (and with it the need for more detailed investigations of both) is increased.

CONCLUSIONS

In recent years, it has become increasingly apparent that, despite major technological advances, the social aspects of organization remain of

136

critical importance, and thus a continuing focus for managerial (and academic) concern. We have attempted to show some of the ways in which time is a key element in the social dimension of organization, and how a more detailed analysis of individual and organizational time might lead to fresh insight into the main processes and experiences of organizational life. In particular, the predominance of rationalization as the guiding principle for work organization needs both conceptual and empirical qualification and investigation. The intensification of worktime has been overshadowed by the gradual overall reduction in work duration.

The principles underlying the broader social structuring of time have been imperfectly examined. The actual duration of worktime is the product of a wide variety of legal, institutional, economic, and social factors, operating through a process of interaction which is, at best, barely understood. Cross-cultural comparisons may expand our understanding. Americans, for example, appear to structure their time more tightly than Europeans because they value activity more than human relations (Hall 1959): the schedule is more important than human interaction so that people are fitted into time-slots. One might argue that Europeans are moving in the same direction. The intensity of worktime is similarly determined. Is the intensification of worktime the natural consequence of time commodification, so that a market economy, with its emphasis on the maximum utilization of scarce resources, leads inexorably to increased pressure on worktime? 'Does the market system apportion time to the uses best fitted to satisfy human needs, as economists argued that it apportioned land, labour and capital?' (Carlstein et al. 1978: 244). The answers to these questions, we have argued, depend ultimately on the conceptualization of time adopted by the questioner. In a very real sense, time is the ultimate scarce resource.

References

Anthony, P.D. (1977), *The Ideology of Work*, London: Tavistock.

Bachelard, G. (1950), *La Dialectique de la durée*, Paris: Presses Universitaires de France.

Ballante, D. and Jackson, M. (1979), *Labour Economics*, New York: McGraw Hill.

Barthes, R. (1975), *Roland Barthes*, Paris: Seuil.

Barzel, Y. (1973), 'The determination of daily hours and wages', *Quarterly Journal of Economics*, vol. 87, pp. 220–38.

Becker, G. S. (1965), 'A theory of the allocation of time', *Economic Journal*, vol. 75, pp. 495–517.

Becker, G.S. (1977), *The Economic Approach to Human Behaviour*, Chicago, London: University of Chicago Press.

Bednaznik, R.W. (1980), 'Work sharing in the US: its prevalence and duration', *Monthly Labor Review*, vol. 103, no. 7, pp. 3–12.

Bensman, J. and Lilienfeld, R. (1973), *Craft and Consciousness: occupational technique and the development of world images*, New York: Wiley-Interscience.

Bergson, H. (1910), *Time and Free Will: an essay on the immediate data of consciousness*, London: Allen & Unwin.

Best, E. (1922), 'The Maori division of time', *Dominion Museum Monograph*, no. 4.

Best, F. (1980), *Flexible Life Scheduling: breaking the education-work-retirement lockstep*, New York: Praeger.

Bienefeld, M.A. (1972), *Working Hours in British Industry an economic history*, London: Weidenfeld & Nicholson.

Blackler, F. and Brown, C. (1978), *Job Redesign and Management Control*, Farnborough: Saxon House.

Blandy, A. (1984), 'New technology and flexible patterns of working time', *Employment Gazette*, vol. 92, no. 10, pp. 439–44.

Blaug, M. (1976), 'The empirical status of human capital theory: a slightly jaundiced survey', *Journal of Economic Literature*, vol. 14, no. 3 (September), pp. 827–55.

Blauner, R. (1964), *Alienation and Freedom: the factory worker and his industry*, Chicago, London: University of Chicago Press.

Blyton, P. (1982) 'The industrial relations of work-sharing', *Industrial Relations Journal*, vol. 13, no. 3, pp. 6–12.

—— (1984), 'Partial Retirement: some insights from the Swedish partial pension scheme', *Ageing and Society*, vol. 4, no. 1, pp. 69–83.

—— (1985), *Changes in Working Time: an international review*, London: Croom Helm.

—— (1987), 'The working-time debate in western Europe', *Industrial Relations*, vol. 26, no. 2, pp. 201-7.

—— (1989a), 'Hours of work', in R. Bean (ed.), *International Labour Statistics*, London: Routledge, in press.

—— (1989b), *Time under Capitalism*, London: Macmillan.

Blyton, P. and Hill, S. (1981) 'The economics of worksharing', *National Westminster Bank Quarterly Review*, no. 136, pp. 37–45.

Bohannon, P. (1953), 'Concepts of time among the Tiv of Nigeria', *Southwestern Journal of Anthropology*, 9, pp. 251–62.

Bollnow, O.F. (1977), 'Das richtige Verhaltniz zur Zeit', *Confinia Psychiat*, 20, pp. 209–27.

Bolter, J.D. (1984), *Turing's Man: western culture in the computer age*, London: Duckworth.

Bosch, G. (1986a), *Reducing Annual Working Time and Improving Schedule Flexibility — causes, effects, controversies*, Proceedings Vol. 3 International Industrial Relations Association, Seventh World Congress, Hamburg, Federal Republic of Germany, pp. 159–79.

—— (1986b), 'The dispute over the reduction of the working week in West Germany', *Cambridge Journal of Economics*, vol. 10, pp. 271–90.

Bosworth, D.L. and Dawkins, P.J. (1978), 'Proposed changes in the extent and nature of shiftworking', *Personnel Review*, vol. 7, no. 4, pp. 32–5.

—— (1980), 'Shiftworking and unsocial hours', *Industrial Relations Journal*, vol. 11, no. 1, pp. 32–40.

—— (1981), *Work Patterns: an economic analysis*, Aldershot: Gower.

Braverman, H. (1974) *Labour and Monopoly Capital: the degradation of work in the twentieth century*, New York, London: Monthly Review Press.

Brechling, F.P.R. (1965), 'The relationship between output and employment in British manufacturing industries', *Review of Economic Studies*, vol. 47, pp. 187–216.

Brown, C.V., Levin, E.J., Roas, R.J., Ruffell, D.T., and Ulph, H.M. (1984), *Treasury Report: direct taxation and short-run labour supply*, Working Paper no. 18, University of Stirling.

Browne, R.C. (1949), 'The day and night performance of teleprinter switchboard operators', *Occupational Psychology*, vol. 23, pp. 121–6.

Bruner, J.F. (1960), *Process of Education*, Cambridge (Mass): Harvard University Press.

Burrell, G. and Morgan, G. (1979), *Sociological Paradigms and Organizational Analysis*, London: Heinemann.

Burgess, K. (1975), *The Origins of British Industrial Relations: the nineteenth century experience*, London: Croom Helm.

Calkins, K. (1969–70), 'Time: perspectives, marking and styles of usage', *Social Problems*, vol. 20, pp. 487–501.

Carlstein, T., Parkes, D. and Thrift, N. (eds.) (1978), *Timing Space and Spacing Time. Volume 2: human activity and time geography*, London: Edward Arnold.

Carroll, J.F.X. (1979), 'Staff burnout as a form of ecological dysfunction', *Contemporary Drug Problems*, vol. 8, pp. 207–25.

Cavendish, R. (1982), *Women on the Line*, London: Routledge & Kegan Paul.

Chacholiades, M. (1986), *Microeconomics*, New York: Macmillan.

Chandler, A.D. (1977), *The Visible Hand: the managerial revolution in American business*, Cambridge (Mass), London: Harvard University Press.

Clark, P.A. (1978), 'Temporal innovations and time structuring in large organizations', in J.T. Fraser, N. Lawrence, and D. Park (eds.), *The Study of Time: Vol. 3*, New York: Springer-Verlag.

—— (1982), 'A Review of the theories of time and structure for organizational sociology', Working paper no. 248, Management Centre, University of Aston.

Clark, P.A., Hantrais, L., Hassard, J.S., Linhart, D. and Starkey, K.P. (1984), 'The porous day and *temps choisi*', paper presented at the Third Annual 'Organization and Control of the Labour Process' Conference, Aston University, England.

Clark, P.A. and Starkey, K.P. (1988), *Organizational Transitions and Innovation-Design*, London: Pinter.

Codrington, R.H. (1891), *The Melanesians*, Oxford.

Cohen, J. (1968), 'Subjective time', in Fraser, J.T. (ed.), *The Voices of Time*, Harmondsworth: Penguin.

Cohen, S. and Taylor, L. (1972), *Psychological Survival: the experience of long-term imprisonment*, Harmondsworth: Penguin.

Colquhoun, W.P. (1970), 'Circadian rhythms, mental efficiency and shift work', *Ergonomics*, vol. 13, pp. 558–60.

Colquhoun, W.P., Blake, M.J., and Edwards, R.S. (1968), 'Experimental studies of shift work 1: a comparison of "rotating" and "stabilized" four-hour shift systems', *Ergonomics*, vol. 11, pp. 427–53.

Cooper, C.L. and Marshall, J. (1976), 'Occupational sources of stress: a review of the literature relating to coronary heart disease and mental ill-health', *Journal of Occupational Psychology*, vol. 49, pp. 11–28.

Cottrell, W.F. (1939), 'Of time and the railroader', *American Journal of Sociology*, vol. 4, pp. 190–8.

Csikzentmihalyi, M. (1975), *Beyond Boredom and Anxiety*, San Francisco, London: Jossey-Bass.

Davis, F. (1963) *Passage Through Crisis*, Indianapolis: Bobbs-Merrill.

Denison, E.F. (1962) 'The sources of economic growth and the alternatives before the US', Supplementary Paper 13, New York: Committee for Economic Development.

DeSerpa, A.C. (1971), 'A theory of the economics of time', *Economic Journal* (December), vol. 81, pp. 828–46.

Desmons, G. and Vidal-Hall, T. (1987), *Annual Hours*, London: Industrial Society.

Diamant, A. (1970), 'The temporal dimension in models of administration and organization', in D. Waldo (ed.), *Temporal Dimensions of Development Administration*, Durham (North Carolina): Duke University Press.

Dickson, P. (1975), *Work Revolution*, London: Allen & Unwin.

Ditton, J. (1979), 'Baking time', *Sociological Review*, vol. 27, pp. 157–67.

Dunham, J. (1980), 'An exploratory study of staff stress in English and German comprehensive schools', *Educational Review*, vol. 32, pp. 11–20.

Durkheim, E. (1976), *The Elementary Forms of the Religious Life*, London: George Allen & Unwin, Second Edition.

Edwards, R.C. (1979), *Contested Terrain: the transformation of the workplace in the twentieth century*, London: Heinemann.

EIRR (European Industrial Relations Review) (1987), 'Working time in seventeen countries', *European Industrial Relations Review*, no. 158, pp. 18–26.

Eliade, M. (1959), *Cosmos and History: the myth of the eternal return*, New York: Harper & Row.

Emery, F. and Trist, E. (1965), *Towards a Social Ecology*, New York: Plenum.

Etzioni, A. (1961), *A Comparative Analysis of Complex Organizations*, New York: Free Press.

ETUI (European Trade Union Institute) (1979), *The Reduction of Working Time in Western Europe: Part 1*, Brussels: ETUI.

—— (1984), *Practical Experiences with the Reduction of Working Time in Western Europe*, Brussels: ETUI.

Evans, A.A. (1969), 'Work and leisure 1919–69', *International Labour Review*, vol. 99, no. 1, pp. 35–9.

—— (1975), *Hours of Work in Industrialised Countries*, Geneva: International Labour Office.

Evans, A. and Palmer, S. (1985), *Negotiating Shorter Working Hours*, London: Macmillan.

Evans-Pritchard, E.E. (1940), *The Nuer*, Oxford: Oxford University Press.

Fairbrother, P. (1987), 'Restructuring production and union renewal: Japanization in process?', paper presented to a conference entitled 'The Japanization of British Industry' at the University of Wales Institute of Science and Technology, September.

Farber, M.L. (1953), 'Time-perception and feeling-tone: a study in the perception of the days', *Journal of Psychology*, vol. 35, pp. 253–7.

Feldstein, M.S. (1967), 'Specification of labour input in the aggregate production function', *Review of Economic Studies*, vol. 34, pp. 375–86.

Fenton, S. (1984), *Durkheim and Modern Sociology*, Cambridge: Cambridge University Press.

Ferner, A. (1985), 'Political constraints and management strategies: The case of working practices in British Rail', *British Journal of Industrial Relations*, vol. 23, no. 1, pp. 47–70.

Filipcova, B. and Filipec, J. (1986), 'Society and concepts of time', *International Social Science Journal*, no. 107, pp. 19–32.

Finn, P. (1981), 'The effects of shiftwork on the lives of employees', *Monthly Labour Review*, vol. 104, no. 10, pp. 31–5.

Flanders, A. (1964), *The Fawley Productivity Agreements*, London: Faber.

Foss, M. (1963), 'The utilisation of capital equipment: postwar compared with prewar', *Survey of Current Business*, (June) vol. 43, no. 6, pp. 8–16.

Friedrich, R.W. (1970), *A Sociology of Sociology*, New York: New York Free Press.

Fraisse, P. (1964), *The Psychology of Time*, London: Eyre & Spottiswoode.

Frankenhaeuser, M. and Gardell, B. (1976), 'Underload and overload in working life: outline of a multidisciplinary approach', *Journal of Human Stress*, vol. 2, pp. 35–46.

Fraser, J.T. (ed.) (1968), *The Voices of Time*, Harmondsworth: Penguin.

French, J.R.P., Caplan, R.O. and van Harrison, R. (1982), *The Mechanism of Job Stress and Strain*, Chichester: Wiley.

Friedman, M. and Rosenman, R.H. (1974), *Type A Behavior and Your Heart*, London: Wildwood House.

Fudge, C. (1980), 'Night and day', *Employment Gazette*, vol. 88, no. 10, pp. 1120–3.

Gallie, D. (1978), *In Search of the New Working Class: automation and social integration within the capitalist enterprise*, Cambridge: Cambridge University Press.

141

Gearing, E. (1958), 'The structural poses of the 18th century Cherokee villages', *American Anthropologist*, vol. 60, pp. 1148–57.

Gerber, L.A. (1983), *Married to their Careers: careers and family dilemmas in doctors' lives*, London: Tavistock.

Gesell, A.L. and Ilg, F.C. (1943), *Infant and Child in the Culture of Today*, New York: Harper.

Ghez, G. and Becker, G.S. (1975), *The Allocation of Time and Goods over the Life Cycle*, New York: NBER

Giddens, A. (1979), *Central Problems in Social Theory*, London: Macmillan.

—— (1981), *A Contemporary Critique of Historical Materialism, Volume 1: power, property and the state*, London: Macmillan.

—— (1984), *The Constitution of Society*, Cambridge: Cambridge University Press.

Gioscia, V. (1972), 'On social time', in H. Yaker, H. Osmond, and F. Cheek (eds.), *The Future of Time*, New York: Anchor Books.

—— (1974), *Time Forms*, New York: Gordon & Breach.

Glaser, B.G. and Strauss, A. (1965), 'Temporal Aspects of Dying', *American Journal of Sociology*, vol. 71, pp. 48–59.

Glasser, R. (1972) *Time in French Life and Thought*, Manchester: Manchester University Press.

Gouldner, A. (1955), 'Metaphysical pathos and the theory of bureaucracy', *American Political Science Review*, vol. 49, pp. 496–507.

Graham, R.J. (1981), 'The perception of time in consumer research', *Journal of Consumer Research*, vol. 7, pp. 335–42.

Grazia, S. de (1972), 'Time and work', in H. Yaker, H. Osmond, and F. Cheek (eds.), *The Future of Time*, New York: Anchor Books.

—— (1974), *Of Time, Work, and Leisure*, New York: Anchor Books.

Gronau, R. (1977), 'Leisure, home production and work — the theory of the allocation of time revisited', *Journal of Political Economy*, vol. 85, pp. 1099–123.

Grossin, W. (1969), *Le Travail et le Temps: horaires-durées-rhythmes*, Paris and La Haye: Editions Anthropos.

—— (1974), *Les Temps de la Vie Quotidienne*, Paris, La Haye: Mouton.

Gulowsen, J. (1972), 'A measure of work group autonomy', in L. Davis and J. Taylor (eds.), *Design of Jobs*, Harmondsworth: Penguin, pp. 374–90.

Gundersen, E.K.E. and Rahe, R.H. (eds.) (1974), *Life Stress and Illness*, Springfield, Illinois: Charles C. Thomas.

Gunnell, J.G. (1970), 'Development, social change and time', in Waldo, D. (ed.), *Temporal Dimensions of Development Administration*, Durham (North Carolina): Duke University Press.

Gurdon, P.T.R. (1914), *The Khasis*, London.

Gurvitch, G. (1964), *The Spectrum of Social Time*, Dordrecht: D. Reidel.

Hadfield, R.A. and Gibbins, H. de B. (1982), *A Shorter Working Day*, London: Methuen.

Hall, E.T. (1959), *The Silent Language*, New York: Doubleday.

Hanami, T. (1980), *Labor Relations in Japan Today*, London: John Martin.

Hanley, J.R. and Morris, N. (1982), 'Time estimation as a function of recall: a test of Ornstein's theory of temporal judgement', *Current Psychological Research*, vol. 2, pp. 45–54.

Harris, J. (1972), *Unemployment and Politics: a Study in English social policy*, Oxford, Clarendon.

Harrison, M. (1986), 'The ordering of the urban environment: time, work and the occurrence of crowds', *Past and Present*, no. 110, pp. 134–68.

Hart, R.A. (1984), *The Economics of Non-wage Labour Costs*, London: Allen & Unwin.

—— (1987), *Working Time and Employment*, London: Allen & Unwin.

Harton, J.J. (1939), 'An investigation of the influence of success and failure on the estimation of time', *Journal of General Psychology*, vol. 21, pp. 51–62.

Heath, L.R. (1956), *The Concept of Time*, Chicago: University of Chicago Press.

Hedges, J.N. and Taylor, D.E. (1980), 'Recent trends in worktime', *Monthly Labor Review*, vol. 103, no. 3, pp. 3–11.

Heirich, M. (1964), 'The use of time in the study of social change', *American Sociological Review*, vol. 29, pp. 386–97.

Hicks, J.R. (1932), *The Theory of Wages*, New York: Macmillan.

Hill, S. (1981), *Competition and Control at Work*, London: Heinemann.

Hill, S. (1984), *Worksharing: some cost and other implications*, London, Unemployment Unit.

—— (1987), 'Working time changes and employment growth', *Lloyds Bank Review*, January, no. 163, pp. 31–46.

—— (1989), *Managerial Economics*, London: Macmillan.

Hill, S. and Blyton, P. (1987), 'Flexibility and patterns of work', paper presented to a conference entitled 'The Japanization of British Industry', at the University of Wales Institute of Science and Technology, September.

Hinrichs, K., Roche, W.K., and Wiesenthal, H. (1985), 'Working time policy as class oriented strategy: unions and shorter working hours in Great Britain and West Germany', *European Sociological Review*, vol. 1, no. 3, pp. 211–29.

Hodson, T.C. (1908), *The Meitheis*, London.

Hubert, H. (1905), 'Etude sommaire de la representation du temps dans la religion et la magie', *Annuaire de l'Ecole Pratique des Hautes Etudes*, pp. 1–39.

Hubert, H. and Mauss, M. (1909), *Mélanges d'Histoire des Religions*, Paris: Alcan.

Hughes, E.C. (1971), *The Sociological Eye*, New York: Aldine.

IDS (Incomes Data Services) (1987), *European Report*, no. 289, London: IDS

ILO (International Labour Organization) (1978), *Management of Working Time in Industrialised Countries*, Geneva: ILO.

—— (1984), *Working Time: reduction of hours of work, weekly rest and holidays with pay*, Geneva: ILO.

Isambert, F-A. (1979), 'Henri Hubert et la sociologie du temps', *Revue Française de Sociologie*, vol. 20, pp. 183–204.

Jaques, E. (1976), *A General Theory of Bureaucracy*, London: Halsted Heinemann.

—— (1982), *The Form of Time*, London: Heinemann.

Jahoda, M. Lasarsfeld, P.F. and Zeisel, H. (1972), *Marienthal: the sociology of an unemployed community*, London: Tavistock.

Jahoda, M. (1979), 'The Impact of unemployment in the 1930s and the 1970s', *Bulletin of the British Psychological Society*, vol. 32, pp. 309–14.

143

Jenkins, C. and Sherman, B. (1979), *The Collapse of Work*, London: Eyre Methuen.

Judkins, P. West, D. and Drew, J. (1985), *Networking in Organizations: the Rank Xerox experiment*, Aldershot: Gower.

Julkunnen, R.A. (1977), 'A contribution to the categories of social time and the economies of time', *Acta Sociologica*, vol. 20, pp. 5–24.

Kahn, R.L., Wolfe, D.M., Quinn, R.P., Snoek, J.D. and Rosenthal, R.A. (1964), *Organizational Stress: studies in role conflict and ambiguity*, New York: Wiley.

Kanter, R. (1984), *The Change Masters*, London: Allen & Unwin.

Kats, R. and Goldberg, A.I. (1982), 'Working extra hours: worker involvement in the modern era, *Personnel Review*, vol. 11, no. 1, pp. 31–4.

Kelly, G.A. (1955), *The Psychology of Personal Constructs*, New York: Norton.

Kern, S. (1983), *The Culture of Time and Space, 1880–1918*, London: Weidenfeld & Nicolson.

Kinchin-Smith, M. and Palmer, S. (1981), 'Getting to the bottom of overtime', *Personnel Management*, February, pp. 27–31.

Kotaro, T. (1980), 'The effect of reductions in working hours on productivity', in S. Nishikawa (ed.), *The Labor Market in Japan*, Tokyo: University of Tokyo Press.

Koutsoyiannis, A. (1975), *Modern Microeconomics*, London: Macmillan.

Kroeber, A.L. (1923), *Anthropology*, New York.

Kuznets, S. (1933), *Seasonal Variations in Industry and Trade*, New York: National Bureau of Economic Research.

Lakoff, G. and Johnson, M. (1980), *Metaphors We Live By*, Chicago: University of Chicago Press.

Lamour, P. and de Chalendar, J. (1974), *Prendre le Travail de Vivre: travail, vacances et retraite à la carte*, Paris: le Seuil.

Landes, D.S. (1983), *Revolution in Time: clocks and the making of the modern world*, Cambridge (Mass): Belknap Press of Harvard University Press.

Laslett, P. (1965), *The World We Have Lost*, London: Methuen.

Lauer, R.H. (1980), *Temporal Man*, New York: Praeger.

Lehmann, P. (1980), 'The National Institute For Occupational Safety and Health: expanding the frontiers of knowledge', in J. MacLaury (ed.), *Protecting People at Work*, Washington: US Department of Labor.

Lewis, J.D. and Weigart, A.J. (1981), 'The structures and meanings of social time', *Social Forces*, vol. 60, pp. 432–62.

Linder, S.B. (1970), *The Harried Leisure Class*, New York, London: Columbia University Press.

Lindsay, C.M. (1971), 'On measuring human capital returns', *Journal of Political Economy*, vol. 79, August.

Littler, C. (1982), *The Development of the Labour Process in Capitalist Societies*, London: Heinemann.

Long, C.L. (1958), *The Labour Force Under Changing Income and Employment*, Princeton: Princeton University Press.

Lukacs, G. (1971), *History and Class Consciousness: studies in Marxist dialectics*, London: Merlin Press.

Lynch, K. (1972), *What Time Is This Place?*, Cambridge (Mass): Massachusetts Institute of Technology Press.

Lynch, P. (1985), 'Annual hours: an idea whose time has come', *Personnel Management*, November, pp. 46–50.

Maanen, J. van and Katz, R. (1979), 'Police perceptions of their environment', *Sociology of Work and Occupations*, vol. 6, pp. 31–58.

McGrath, J.E. and Rotchford, N.L. (1983), 'Time and behaviour in organizations', *Research in Organizational Behaviour*, vol. 5, pp. 57–101.

McKendrick, N. (1962), 'Josiah Wedgwood and the factory discipline', *The Historical Journal*, vol. 4, pp. 30–5.

McKenna, F. (1980), *The Railway Workers 1840–1970*, London: Faber.

Mann, T. (1967), *Memoirs*, London: MacGibbon & Kee.

Manning, P. (1979), 'Metaphors of the field', *Administrative Science Quarterly*, vol. 24, pp. 660–71.

March, J.G. and Simon, H.A. (1958), *Organizations*, New York: Wiley.

Marks, S.R. (1977), 'Multiple roles and role strain: some notes on human energy, time and commitment', *American Sociological Review*, vol. 42, pp. 921–36.

Marris, R. (1964), *The Economics of Capital Utilisation: a report on multiple shiftwork*, Cambridge: Cambridge University Press.

Marx, K. (1976), *Capital*, Volume 1, Harmondsworth: Penguin.

Marx, K. and Engels, F. (1976), *Collected Works*, Volume 6, London: Lawrence & Wishart.

Mauss, M. (1966), *Sociologie et Anthropologie*, Paris: Presses Universitaires de France.

Medawar, P. (1982), 'Type A behaviour and your heart', in *Pluto's Republic*, Oxford: Oxford University Press.

Meier, A. and Rudwick, E. (1978), *Black Detroit and the Rise of the UAW*, New York: Oxford University Press.

Meisel, H. (1984), 'The pioneers: STC in the Federal Republic of Germany', in R. MaCoy and M. Morand (eds.), *Short Time Compensation: a formula for worksharing*, New York: Pergamon.

Merton, R.K. (1940), 'Bureaucratic structure and personality', *Social Forces*, vol. 18, pp. 560–8.

Michael, R. and Becker, G.S. (1973), 'On the new theory of consumer behaviour', *Swedish Journal of Economics*, vol. 75, December, pp. 378–96.

Miles, R. (1980), *Macro Organizational Behaviour*, New York: Goodyear.

Miller, J.G. (1977), 'The nature of living systems', *Behavioral Science*, vol. 16, pp. 277–301.

Minkowski, E. (1970), *Lived Time, Phenomenological and Psychopathological Studies*, Evanston (Illinois): Northwestern University Press.

Mintzberg, H. (1973), *The Nature of Managerial Work*, New York, London: Harper & Row.

Moore, W.E. (1963a), *Man, Time and Society*, New York. Wiley.

—— (1963b), 'The temporal structure of organizations', in E.A. Tiryakian (ed.), *Sociological Theory, Values and Sociocultural Change*, London: Free Press.

Morgan, G. (1986), *Images of Organization*, New York: Sage.

Mumford, L. (1934), *Technics and Civilisation*, New York: Harcourt, Brace & World.

—— (1973), *Interpretations and Forecasts*, New York: Harcourt, Brace, Jovanovich.

Naville, P. (1969), 'Introduction' to W. Grossin, *Le travail et la Temps: horaires-durées-rhythmes*, Paris: Editions Anthropos.

NBPI (National Board for Prices and Incomes) (1970), *Hours of Work, Overtime and Shiftworking*, report no. 161, Cmnd. 4554, London: Her Majesty's Stationery Office.

Nilsonn, P. (1920), *Primitive Time Reckoning*, London: Oxford University Press.

Nowotny, H. (1976), 'Time Structuring and Time Measurement', in J.T. Fraser and N. Lawrence (eds.), *The Study of Time*, vol. 2, New York: Springer-Verlag.

Orme, J.E. (1969), *Time, Experience and Behaviour*, London: Iliffe.

Ornstein, R.E. (1969), *On the Experience of Time*, Harmondsworth: Penguin.

Osborn, D. and Blyton, P. (1985), 'Contrasting Perspectives on productivity bargaining', *Journal of General Management*, vol. 10, no. 3, pp. 65–78.

Owen, J.D. (1976), 'Workweeks and Leisure: an analysis of trends, 1948–75', *Monthly Labour Review*, vol. 99, August, pp. 3–8.

—— (1979), *Working Hours: an economic analysis*, Lexington, (Mass): Heath.

Pahl, J.M. and Pahl, R.E. (1971), *Managers and their Wives*, London: Allen & Unwin.

Parsons, T. (1937), *The Structure of Social Action*, Chicago: Free Press.

Patten, T.H. (1986), *Trends in hours and working time arrangements in the USA*, Proceedings, vol. 3, International Industrial Relations Association Seventh World Congress, Hamburg, Federal Republic of Germany.

Pinder, C. (1982), 'Controlling tropes in administrative science', *Administrative Science Quarterly*, vol. 27, pp. 641–52.

Pinder, C. and Moore, L. (1979), 'The resurrection of taxonomy to aid the development of middle range theories of organization behaviour', *Administrative Science Quarterly*, vol. 24, pp. 99–118.

Pittendrigh, C.S. (1972), 'On mental organization in living systems', in H. Yaker, H. Osmond, and F. Cheek (eds.), *The Future of Time*, New York: Anchor Books.

Pollard, S. (1963),'Factory discipline in the industrial revolution', *Economic History Review*, vol. 16, pp. 254–71.

Poole, M., Mansfield, R., Blyton, P., and Frost, P. (1981), *Managers in Focus*, Aldershot: Gower.

Pronovost, G. (1986), 'Time in a sociological and historical perspective', *International Social Science Journal*, no. 107, pp. 5–18.

Pugh, D.S. *et al.* (1975), *Research in organizational behaviour: a British survey*, London: Heinemann Educational.

Reid, D.A. (1976), 'The decline of Saint Monday', *Past and Present*, no. 71, pp. 76–101.

Reid, F. (1982), 'UI-assisted worksharing as an alternative to layoffs: the Canadian experience', *Industrial and Labor Relations Review*, vol. 35, no. 3, pp. 319–29.

Reid, F. and Meltz, N.M. (1984), 'Canada's STC: a comparison with the California version', in R. McCoy and M. Morand (eds.), *Short-Time Compensation: a formula for worksharing*, New York: Pergamon.

Reyna, R. (1971), 'Metaphysics of time in Indian philosophy and its relevance

146

to practical science', in J. Zeman (ed.), *Time in Science and Philosophy*, Prague: Academia.

Robbins, L. (1930), 'On the elasticity of income in terms of effort', *Economica*, vol. 10, pp.1 23-9.

Roberts, C. (1985), *Harmonization: whys and wherefores*, London: Institute of Personnel Management.

Robertso, I.T. and Smith, M. (1985), *Motivation and Job Design: theory, research and practice*, London: Institute of Personnel Management.

Robinson, J.P. (1977), *How Americans Use Time: a social psychological analysis of everyday behavior*, New York: Praeger.

Robinson, J.P. and Converse, P.E. (1967), *66 Basic Tables of Time Budget Research Data for the US*, Ann Arbor: University of Michigan Press.

Roeber, R. (1973), *The Organization in a Changing Environment*, London: Addison-Wesley.

Rose, M. (1982), *Industrial Behaviour*, London: Penguin Education.

Roth, J.A. (1963), *Timetables: structuring the passage of time in hospital treatment and other careers*, New York: Bobbs-Merrill.

Roy, D.F. (1960), 'Banana time: job satisfaction and informal interaction', in G. Salaman and K. Thompson (eds.), (1973), *People and Organizations*, London: Longmans.

Schonberger, R. (1982), *Japanese Manufacturing Techniques*, New York: Harper & Row.

Schuller, T. (1986), *Age, Capital and Democracy*, Aldershot: Gower.

Selznick, P. (1949), *TVA and the Grass Roots*, Berkley: University of California Press.

Sharp, C. (1981), *The Economics of Time*, Oxford: Martin Robertson.

Sherwood, F. (1970), 'Leadership, organizations and time', in D. Waldo (ed.), *Temporal Dimensions of Development Administration*, Durham (North Carolina); Duke University Press.

Shimada, H. and Hayami, H. (1986), *Working hours and the revision of the labor standards law in Japan*, Proceedings, vol. 3, International Industrial Relations Association Seventh World Congress, Hamburg, Federal Republic of Germany.

Simmel, G. (1903), 'The metropolis and mental life', in *On Individuality and Social Forms*, 1971, Chicago, London: University of Chicago Press.

Smith, M.F. (1982), 'Bloody time and bloody scarcity: capitalism, authority and the transformation of temporal experience in a Papua New Guinea village', *American Ethnologist*, vol. 9, pp. 503-18.

Solovyov, L. (1962), 'The reduction of employees' working hours in the Soviet Union', *International Labour Review*, vol. 86, no. 1, pp. 31-41.

Sorokin, P.A. (1943), *Sociocultural Causality, Space and Time*, Durham (North Carolina): Duke University Press.

Sorokin, P.A. and Merton, R.K. (1937), 'Social time: a methodological and functional analysis', *American Journal of Sociology*, vol. 42, pp. 615-29.

Soule, G. (1956), *What Automation Does to Human Beings*, London: Sedgwick & Jackson.

Standing, G. (1986), 'Meshing labour flexibility with security: an answer to British unemployment?', *International Labour Review*, vol. 125, no. 1, pp. 87-106.

Starkey, K.P. (1988a), 'Time and the labour process: a theoretical and empirical analysis', paper presented at the Aston University (University of Manchester Institute of Science and Technology) Labour Process Conference, Aston.

—— (1988b), 'Time and professional work in public sector organisations', Ph.D. thesis, Aston University.

—— (1988a), 'The consultant's contract, time and professionalism', to appear in R. Frankenberg (ed.), *Time and Health*, London: Routledge & Kegan Paul.

—— (1988b), 'Time and work organisation: a theoretical and empirical analysis', to appear in M. Young and T. Schuller (eds.), *The Rythms of Society*, London: Routledge & Kegan Paul.

Starkey, K.P. and Walsgrove, D. (1985), 'How unemployed youth cope with time', *Occupational Psychology Newsletter*, **18**, 67–9.

Starkey, K.P. and McKinlay, A. (1988), 'Competitive strategies and work organization: emerging patterns of organizational change', *Organization Studies* (forthcoming).

Stigler, G. and Kindahl, J.K. (1970), *The Behaviour of Industrial Prices*, New York: NBER.

Symons, A. (1978), 'Varied working hours — here to stay?', *Work and People*, vol. 4, no. 1/2, pp. 5–12.

Swingle, P. (1976), *The Management of Power*, New York: Wiley.

Szalai, A. (ed.) (1972), *The Use of Time*, The Hague: Mouton.

TUC (Trades Union Congress) (1981), *Report*, London: TUC.

Taylor, F.W. (1911), *Principles of Scientific Management*, New York: Harper.

Thompson, E.P. (1967), 'Time, work-discipline and industrial capitalism', *Past and Present*, vol. 38, pp. 56–97.

Thompson, J.D. (1967), *Organizations in Action*, New York: McGraw-Hill.

Thrift, N. (1981), 'Owners' time and own time: the making of a capitalist time consciousness 1300–1800', in *Space, Time and Geography: essays dedicated to Torgen Hagerstrand*, Lund: CWK Gleesup.

Tinker, T. (1986), 'Metaphor or reification?', *Journal of Management Studies*, vol. 23, pp. 363–84.

Trade Union Research Unit (1981), *Working Time in Britain*, London: Anglo German Foundation.

Treu, T. (1986), *New Trends in Working Time Arrangements*, vol. 3, Proceedings, International Industrial Relations Association Seventh World Congress, Hamburg, Federal Republic of Germany.

Upton, R. (1982), 'Wage costs in crisis: how the Post Office responded', *Personnel Management*, vol. 14, no. 12, pp. 30–34.

Vanek, J. (1973), 'Time spent in housework', *Scientific American*, N.S., vol. 231, November, pp. 116–20.

Visser, J. (1986), *New working time arrangements in the Netherlands*, vol. 3, Proceedings, International Industrial Relations Association Seventh World Congress, Hamburg, Federal Republic of Germany.

Voogd, L. (1978), 'Shiftwork in the Netherlands', in ILO *Management of Working-Time in Industrialised Countries*, ILO, Geneva.

Webb, S. and Cox, H. (1891), *The Eight Hours Day*, London: Scott.

Weber, M. (1952), *The Protestant Ethic and the Spirit of Capitalism*, London: Allen & Unwin.

White, M. (1980), *Shorter Working Time*, Report No. 589, London: Policy Studies Institute.

—— (1982), *Shorter Working Hours Through National Industry Agreements*, Department of Employment Research Paper No. 38, London: Her Majesty's Stationery Office.

White, M. and Ghobadian, A. (1984), *Shorter Working Hours in Practice*, Report no. 631, London: Policy Studies Institute.

Whybrew, E.G. (1968), *Overtime Working in Britain*, Research Paper 9, Royal Commission on Trade Unions and Employers' Associations, London: Her Majesty's Stationery Office.

Winch, P. (1958), *The Idea of a Social Science*, London: Routledge & Kegan Paul.

Winston, G.C. (1974), 'The theory of capital utilisation and idleness', *Journal of Economic Literature*, vol. 12, no. 4, (December), pp. 1301–20.

Wright, L. (1968), *Clockwork Man*, London: Elek.

Zerubavel, E. (1976), 'Timetables and scheduling: on the social organization of time', *Sociological Inquiry*, vol. 46, pp. 87–94.

—— (1979), *Patterns of Time in Hospital Life*, Chicago: University of Chicago Press.

—— (1981), *Hidden Rhythms: schedules and calendars in social life*, Chicago: Chicago University Press.

Subject Index

Author Index

For Product Safety Concerns and Information please contact our EU
representative GPSR@taylorandfrancis.com Taylor & Francis Verlag GmbH,
Kaufingerstraße 24, 80331 München, Germany

Printed and bound by CPI Group (UK) Ltd, Croydon, CR0 4YY
08/05/2025
01864454-0002